New Directions for Adult and Continuing Education

Susan Imel
Jovita M. Ross-Gordon
COEDITORS-IN-CHIEF

Decentering the Ivory Tower of Academia

Dianne Ramdeholl
EDITOR

Number 139 • Fall 2013
Jossey-Bass
San Francisco

DECENTERING THE IVORY TOWER OF ACADEMIA
Dianne Ramdeholl (ed.)
New Directions for Adult and Continuing Education, no. 139
Susan Imel, Jovita M. Ross-Gordon, Coeditors-in-Chief

Microfilm copies of issues and articles are available in 16mm and 35mm, as well as microfiche in 105mm, through University Microfilms Inc., 300 North Zeeb Road, Ann Arbor, Michigan 48106-1346.

NEW DIRECTIONS FOR ADULT AND CONTINUING EDUCATION (ISSN 1052-2891, electronic ISSN 1536-0717) is part of The Jossey-Bass Higher and Adult Education Series and is published quarterly by Wiley Subscription Services, Inc., A Wiley Company, at Jossey-Bass, One Montgomery Street, Suite 1200, San Francisco, CA 94104-4594. POSTMASTER: Send address changes to New Directions for Adult and Continuing Education, Jossey-Bass, One Montgomery Street, Suite 1200, San Francisco, CA 94104-4594.

New Directions for Adult and Continuing Education is indexed in CIJE: Current Index to Journals in Education (ERIC); Contents Pages in Education (T&F); ERIC Database (Education Resources Information Center); Higher Education Abstracts (Claremont Graduate University); and Sociological Abstracts (CSA/CIG).

INDIVIDUAL SUBSCRIPTION RATE (in USD): $89 per year US/Can/Mex, $113 rest of world; institutional subscription rate: $311 US, $351 Can/Mex, $385 rest of world. Single copy rate: $29. Electronic only–all regions: $89 individual, $311 institutional; Print & Electronic–US: $98 individual, $357 institutional; Print & Electronic–Canada/Mexico: $98 individual, $397 institutional; Print & Electronic–Rest of World: $122 individual, $431 institutional.

EDITORIAL CORRESPONDENCE should be sent to the Coeditors-in-Chief, Susan Imel, 3076 Woodbine Place, Columbus, Ohio 43202-1341, e-mail: imel.l@osu.edu; or Jovita M. Ross-Gordon, Southwest Texas State University, CLAS Dept., 601 University Drive, San Marcos, TX 78666.

Cover photograph by Jack Hollingsworth@Photodisc

www.josseybass.com

CONTENTS

EDITOR'S NOTES

For many the academy has historically represented privilege and intellectual exclusion (primarily Eurocentric, White, and male); for others it has represented an increasingly contested site, as marginalized populations have challenged the myth of the ivory tower being a haven of meritocracy and equal opportunities (Wagner, Acker, & Mayuzumi, 2008). Still others persist in viewing universities as a level playing field, a place where people are judged primarily by their ideas and intellectual contributions.

Ironically, alongside these charged conversations of exclusivity, privilege, and lack of access have been the ways in which the ivory tower has been seduced by market interests, sacrificing standards in the interests of efficiency. Much has been written on the ways in which the academy has succumbed to the increasingly market-driven culture of higher education, which has resulted in its commodification and instrumentalization (Faust, 2009; Giroux, 2009). Academic content and new programs are increasingly driven by neoliberal economic interests. This has resulted in reduced state funding of public universities, resulting in a widening gap of costs. The academy's response has generally been to raise tuition (placing the burden on students' shoulders, which has resulted in many students racking up endless debt) and to enter into partnerships with private industries who can influence research agendas in benign and insidious ways by hiring more and more adjuncts who are more expendable and unable to challenge policies in substantive ways. In essence, the haughty ivory tower has been seduced by the flashy neoliberal stranger.

Now added to the ivory tower is the market-driven tower that many have called the most dangerous ideology of the current historical moment. By sabotaging contradictions between democracy and market fundamentalism, and by dismissing social visions as hopelessly out-of-date, theoretical paradigms linking learning to social change have been destroyed (Giroux, 2009).

Yet within this landscape there have been scholars willing to make space to critically interrogate higher education in relation to multiple systems of oppression working to introduce new perspectives, nurturing counter-hegemonic knowledges (Magnusson, 2010). Many, including the authors in this volume, have struggled to cocreate and sustain democratic spheres that decenter dominant interests, with the aim of a more equitable society. They have been part of a larger movement of academic warriors, academics with consciences who live out their commitments by subscribing to the notion that scholarship and activism are inextricably intertwined. They believe that theory is a living document, one that resides in everyday lived realities. This volume embodies their narratives.

As everyday participants in the academy, they are ever mindful to the various ways that knowledge is produced and disseminated and for whom.

NEW DIRECTIONS FOR ADULT AND CONTINUING EDUCATION, no. 139, Fall 2013 © 2013 Wiley Periodicals, Inc.
Published online in Wiley Online Library (wileyonlinelibrary.com) • DOI: 10.1002/ace.20058

Many in this volume have spoken out against the grain of dominant truths, striving to create safe spaces for and with students and others in and out of the academy. This struggle to nurture and preserve decolonized spaces remains an ongoing challenge, especially in the current era of universities needing (or feeling they need) to remain in good standing with government and corporate funders, which may take a toll on academics who engage the larger critical questions of our time.

In the first chapter, Tannis Atkinson uses her own narrative of being a practitioner as a lens to unpack the exploitative ways statistics are being utilized in adult literacy policy. She connects literacy to larger issues of power, situating policies within broader frameworks of colonizing relations.

Juanita Johnson-Bailey reminds us in Chapter 2 of the ways in which racism is systemic and institutionalized in the United States and discusses how, as a woman of color, she addresses racism in her teaching and learning. She also documents an important chapter in the history of the Adult Education Research Conference regarding solidarity between the African Diaspora and LGBTQ preconferences, considering this struggle to build coalitions that transcend race, part of her responsibility in decentering and recentering academia.

In Chapter 3, Shivaani A. Selvaraj explores ways in which her years as an activist for and with homeless populations has centered and guided her in the academy as she continues her struggle for safe spaces that are critical of whose knowledge is privileged, and the process by which this is determined.

Using two examples of partnerships between community groups and higher education institutions, Tom Heaney in Chapter 4 reflects on why one of the examples failed, and he discusses the powerful potential of participatory partnerships in which the university allows the community to lead.

Continuing this thread of community work in Chapter 5, four adult literacy practitioners, John Garvey, John Gordon, Peter Kleinbard, and Paul Wasserman, outline a collaborative effort to document the past 40 years of adult literacy practice and advocacy in New York City, discussing the shrinking spaces and places for participatory adult literacy education.

In Chapter 6, Mechthild Hart argues that engaged scholars and activist researchers must not ignore the social institutional power differentials between the world of community activism and academia, and that those in positions of relative privilege are responsible for finding ways to turn power into resources for those routinely excluded from it.

Empire College's Labor Center, funded by the International Brotherhood of Electrical Workers, is the focus of Chapter 7 as Sharon Szymanski and Richard Wells describe the Center's philosophy and pedagogy, considering dilemmas that arise when educators seek to work with students on a political educational project of reimagining the world and their roles in it.

Mev Miller in Chapter 8 documents a 4-year participatory research project that led to Women Expanding Literacy Education Action Resource Network (WE LEARN), a vibrant women-centered organization that honors knowledges traditionally and often sidelined.

New Directions for Adult and Continuing Education • DOI: 10.1002/ace

In Chapter 9, the editor, Dianne Ramdeholl, critically reflects on the implications of and challenges of working at the intersections and edges of the academy and community.

In my capacity as editor, I would like to conclude by saying that it is my hope that this volume will support you (whatever your site of practice may be) in reimagining your role in the enormous and essential project of decentering. I hope that you might be inspired to conduct community-engaged research as a way of decentering, or seriously question the conditions (and constructedness of those conditions) in which so many marginalized groups live; that you might critically reflect on the sort of community, society, and world you would want to live in; and that you might commit to asking yourself and others "What do we need to achieve that?"

Dianne Ramdeholl
Editor

References

Faust, D. G. (2009, September 6). The university's crisis of purpose. *The New York Times.* Retrieved from http://www.nytimes.com/2009/09/06/books/review/Faust-t.html

Giroux, H. (2009). Beyond the corporate takeover of higher education: Rethinking educational theory, pedagogy, and policy. In M. Simons, M. Olssen, & M. Peters (Eds.), *Rereading educational policy: Studying the policy agenda of the 21st century?* (pp. 458–477). Rotterdam, The Netherlands: Sense Publishers.

Magnusson, J. (2010). Academic activism and nomadic paths. In J. Newson & C. Polster (Eds.), *Academic callings: The university we have had, now have, and could have* (pp. 170–177). Toronto, Ontario, Canada: Canadian Scholars' Press.

Wagner, A., Acker, S., & Mayuzumi, K. (Eds.). (2008). *Whose university is it anyway? Power and privilege on gendered terrain.* Toronto, Ontario, Canada: Sumach Press.

DIANNE RAMDEHOLL *is an assistant professor of adult education and coordinator of the Master of Arts in Adult Learning program (MAAL) in the School for Graduate Studies, Empire State College, New York.*

1

This introductory chapter reflects on the effects of narrowing research agendas and raises questions about how academic work and activism might be mutually beneficial.

Knowledge, Power, Hope: Activism, Research, and Social Justice

Tannis Atkinson

The title of this issue, "Decentering the Ivory Tower of Academia," draws attention to the fact that for some time universities have been regarded as the legitimate holders of knowledge, and that academic knowledge is, by definition, removed from the "real world." One could argue that adult education has never fit into that mold because of its roots in emancipatory and democratic movements and its struggle for recognition as an academic discipline. Because of its history and position, adult education has been finding ways to build bridges between communities and "the academy" for a very long time. In recognition of this fact, Dianne Ramdeholl organized the opening panel of the 2012 Adult Education Research Conference (AERC) as an opportunity to hear from individuals who were committed to working with marginalized communities and populations. The speakers outlined how, as activists and academics, they have negotiated the chasms between communities and academic institutions. Panelists described what they value in each of these disparate locations and discussed the struggles and dilemmas that arose when they tried to democratize practices and to value diverse ways of knowing. This issue of *New Directions for Adult and Continuing Education* builds on that panel by including all of the speakers, plus several other adult educators committed to democratic practice. Each chapter grapples with some aspect of the complex and contested relationships between communities and the academy, reflecting on whose knowledge counts, and why this matters. The authors describe the vast chasms between activist and academic knowledges but also the fruitful interchanges that can occur, and what material, contextual, and conceptual conditions make it possible—or challenging—to build relationships based on genuine dialogue and mutual respect.

New Directions for Adult and Continuing Education, no. 139, Fall 2013 © 2013 Wiley Periodicals, Inc.
Published online in Wiley Online Library (wileyonlinelibrary.com) • DOI: 10.1002/ace.20059

Why This Issue? Why Now?

We are living through an era in which education at all levels is being transformed. Educators are under pressure to abandon their vision for a more just and equitable world and to consider themselves primarily as technicians whose role is to train individuals to attain predictable, instrumental learning outcomes. These pressures are part of larger forces that have been occurring transnationally, changes that have been accompanied by a rigid insistence that education be based on "evidence-based" research. As many have argued, the move to evidence-based research reasserts a particular research paradigm and privileges very limited forms of evidence (Lather, 2004).

Educational researchers have been raising concerns about the limits of positivist research for some time; its proscription against "untestable explanations" not only constrains "critical educational thought" but also privileges the status quo (Belzer & St. Clair, 2005, p. 1408). Some scholars understand current trends in policy making as related to the commodification of education (Arvast, 2006; Hamilton, 2012; Tusting, 2012) arising from the intensification of capitalism (Allman, 1999; Beach, 2003; Tikly, 2009). Others note how these changes are reinstating historical patterns of dominance (Bannerji, 2005; Castro-Gómez, 2007; Hernandez-Zamora, 2010; Ng & Shan, 2010; Ntiri, 2009). For still others, these changes have emerged from a complex of relations and discourses and are connected to forms of governance that produce particular subjectivities (Fejes & Nicoll, 2008; Fendler, 1998; Peters, Besley, Olssen, Maurer, & Weber, 2009; Popkewitz, 2012). No matter how we understand the reasons for the move to market managerialism in education policy and research, the increased emphasis on evidence-based policy is affecting research, frontline practice, and community–university partnerships. Many educators feel their teaching work is less important than the statistical reports and test results they are expected to produce. These trends are diametrically opposed to the emancipatory, liberatory, or democratic education valued by the authors in this issue. But these activists do not bemoan the limits that exist in the current context. Instead, each chapter explores different facets of the imbalances of power in relationships between communities and academia.

The Case of Adult Literacy. To begin the discussion I will briefly describe how these dilemmas have manifested in adult literacy in Canada, a field in which I have close to three decades of experience. Literacy educators work with the most disadvantaged and marginalized populations; adults who struggle with print tend to be low-income people who have had limited access to education or those whose literacy practices (Street, 2003) are furthest from the norms reflected in the school system. As in the United States, adult literacy has always received substantially fewer resources and supports than any other level of education, and many literacy instructors work part-time for very low pay. Over the past few decades adult literacy work has been transformed by educational statistics.

New Directions for Adult and Continuing Education • DOI: 10.1002/ace

In many advanced liberal nations in the Global North, current adult literacy policies are guided by a narrow form of evidence developed in the United States. In 1989 the National Center for Education Statistics in the United States contracted Educational Testing Services (ETS) to develop and conduct a large-scale assessment. The National Adult Literacy Survey (NALS) used a psychometric approach that built on previous ETS work to quantify the skills of youth and the "literacy proficiencies of job seekers" (Kirsch, Jungeblut, Jenkins, & Kolstad, 2002, p. 2). The NALS framing was extended to an international level when the Department of Education pressured the Organization for Economic Cooperation and Development (OECD) to undertake transnational comparisons that could "help assess the USA's position on the international market" (Cussó & D'Amico, 2005, p. 206). The OECD undertook this work starting with the 1994 International Adult Literacy Survey (IALS) which, according to its designers, offered data that countries could use to develop "lifelong learning, social and labour market policies" (OECD & Statistics Canada, 2000, p. xii).

Critics of these surveys argue that they project a mythical future and posit a universal form of information processing that disregards cultural differences and dismisses individuals' actual uses of literacy (Gomez, 2000; Hamilton & Barton, 2000; Hautecoeur, 2000; Manesse, 2000). Policies based on survey data attempt to manage and standardize the work of community programs through extensive reporting (Hamilton, 2001; Hautecoeur, 1997; LoBianco & Wickert, 2001; Merrifield, 1997); these requirements leave many educators feeling that teaching is less important than producing numerical reports (Crooks et al., 2008; Jackson, 2005). Researchers in England and Canada have found that such accountability demands encourage programs to work with those who can most quickly show progress rather than those facing the greatest barriers (Bathmaker, 2007; Hillier, 2009; Myers & de Broucker, 2006; Smythe, 2011; Veeman, Ward, & Walker, 2006); there is no doubt that the National Reporting System has had similar effects in the United States.

In Canada over the past decade, adult literacy research has become increasingly quantitative and divorced from context or questions arising from practice. One literature review found "a paucity of research on the reading behaviours, strategies and processes of adult literacy learners" (Campbell, 2003, p. 6). Another found that almost 40% of research "focuses on numerical descriptions and analysis of the Canadian population with respect to literacy" (Quigley, Folinsbee, & Kraglund-Gauthier, 2006, p. 16); the authors noted a lack of research on "the lived experiences of adults with literacy challenges, on their learning experiences in programs or tutorial situations, on practitioners' experiences, or on the everyday literacy practices of people with literacy challenges" (p. 26). But this has not always been the case. For about 15 years, between the late 1990s and 2009, adult literacy research was supported by a federal body that explicitly supported a community development approach (Hayes, 2009). Established in 1987, the role of the National Literacy

New Directions for Adult and Continuing Education • DOI: 10.1002/ace

Secretariat (NLS) was to support work that "promote[d] the value of literacy and lifelong learning as primary forces for achieving personal well-being" (National Literacy Secretariat, 1996, p. 5). One mechanism for doing so was to "encourage, enhance, fund and commission literacy research" that would "promote collaboration between researchers, practitioners and learners" (National Literacy Secretariat, 1998, pp. 2–3). In that period Canada had "an international reputation for bringing research and practice together" (St. Clair, 2007, p. 63) because the NLS worked "to use research as a tool for community development—a way to get resources and knowledge to grassroots literacy programs" (p. 59).

I worked for 7 years as editor of *Literacies*, a national journal funded by the NLS that aimed to link research and practice. The journal was established following substantial groundwork that gathered information about reflective practice and research-in-practice (Horsman & Norton, 1999; Quigley & Norton, 2002), initiated practitioner research projects (Niks, Allen, Davies, McRae, & Nonesuch, 2003; Norton & Malicky, 2000), and brought together practitioner–researchers from across the country (Norton & Woodrow, 2001). This work relied on an expansive definition of research, one that included "all of the ways that people . . . look again, articulating and clarifying what they know, and pushing out into the unclear and the unknown" (Darville, 2003, p. 3). Some of this research was done autonomously in community programs, while some was done in partnership with independent researchers or with university faculty and students.

Research connected to practice can ask and explore questions that can strengthen programming and practice. While it flourished, practitioner research was exciting precisely because it asked fundamental questions, such as how to actively decolonize ways of understanding aboriginal literacies (Antone, Gamlin, & Provost-Turchetti, 2003; Balanoff & Chambers, 2005; Silver, Klyne, & Simard, 2003), how to address complex issues such as violence (Horsman, 1999; Norton, 2004) and homelessness (Trumpener, 1997), and why "nonacademic" outcomes are as significant as gains in "skills" (Battell, Gesser, Rose, Sawyer, & Twiss, 2004; Grieve 2003; Wrigley, 2005). Despite its richness, practitioner research has been described as "feral literature" because it is not necessarily widely disseminated and it can be difficult to locate (Horsman & Woodrow, 2006, p. 155).

A national project that was to guide a national framework for research in practice noted that "[a]dult literacy and basic upgrading suffers from a lack of recognition, minimal professional development opportunities, and insufficient funding supports" (Woodrow, 2006, p. 21). In their discussion of the United Kingdom, Scotland, and Ireland, Hamilton and Tett (2012) note that adult literacy educators are "used to working creatively 'in the cracks,' with inadequate funding or formal structures that support the understandings that they have gained from their experience about what good practice entails" (p. 51). Similar conditions prevail in most nations in the Global North. Given these conditions, practitioner research would not be possible without critical supports such as resource centers, networks, or mentors. In Canada the research mentors were affiliated with universities and offered advice, training, and access to resources.

As editor of *Literacies* I knew that such mentorships could be challenging. In some cases community researchers were stung by what they perceived as condescension on the part of university researchers, and academics felt that educators misunderstood or belittled their work. At other times the material differences between literacy programs and universities became a source of tension: While academics are expected to do research, community programs often took on this work as a means to access additional revenue. Since these projects rarely allowed programs to hire more staff, practitioner research entailed further work for educators, leading to exhaustion and burnout. Now that I am immersed in the academic world, I am aware that as a graduate student I have access to many more resources and supports than I did as a worker in a community literacy program. I am extremely privileged to be a doctoral candidate, able to explore a range of perspectives on vital issues, and am reminded that the "ivory tower" remains one of the few spaces in which it is possible to consider broad questions that get pushed aside by the imperatives of practice.

Learning that the pervasive literacy statistics were developed out of a desire to link literacy to economic productivity and competitiveness has helped me make sense of why educators find it increasingly difficult to design programs that start from the lived experiences of the students who attend our programs. The next step for me is to find ways to share what I am learning with the field. As I make plans to do so I realize that what I have learned about the history of statistics may help to set the dilemmas of current practice in a larger context, but does not address the immediate needs of frontline educators. Every day literacy tutors, instructors, and program coordinators are forced to juggle the needs of flesh-and-blood individuals sitting in front of them and the punitive imperatives of contemporary policies. How can I share my findings in ways that won't intensify their dilemmas? While I don't have answers about exactly how my research might be useful, I am committed to doing research that can serve as a resource for strengthening the field and supporting the aspirations of those who are routinely excluded from education and from decision making on all levels. Some of my research has documented how educators work around the demands that force them to objectify the students in the classes they teach. Will publishing this information lead to policies that further tighten the noose on programs that are finding ways to preserve emancipatory values in today's hostile environment? I can't know the impact of all of my choices and actions. None of us can. What we can do is hold onto the principles that guide us and remember that our choices affect people's lives and the future for us all.

Power, Knowledge, and Justice. The example of adult literacy work illustrates that differences between communities and the academy are both material and epistemological. It is worth asking whose interests are served by these disparities. Universities have access to more resources, and are supported by more solid infrastructures than community programs or projects for equity and social justice. The relative stability and power of universities could be a resource for activists, yet very often the interest of the institution outweighs the potential to challenge the status quo. The effects of institutionalization and bureaucratization are a fruitful site for research. Critical reflections on the challenges in university–community partnerships could offer insights about how to proceed and how to transform the partnerships between these very different players. Several chapters in this issue do just that.

Community development approaches to practice and qualitative approaches to research allow for local relevance and evolving understandings. Positivist approaches, on the other hand, require an insistence on limiting what is relevant and focusing only on what can be tested. Past efforts to contest the role and position of academic knowledge have been connected to larger struggles for social justice and transformation. Some challenges have come from people demanding access to an institution that was, for too long, the preserve of White, middle-class men. Other demands have led to transformed research methods and new theoretical frameworks, some of which have meant that academic knowledge has become more relevant to communities. And yet much of what is considered legitimate knowledge continues to fall within the fold of Enlightenment thinking, and non-Eurocentric ways of thinking and knowing continue to be excluded as legitimate knowledge (Mignolo, 2013; Quijano, 2000).

Within communities and academia, some knowledge is more powerful than others, as has become clear with the move to evidence-based policies. Advocates of this approach cite its efficiency and effectiveness, and claim that the evidence offers useful outcomes. Its detractors, on the other hand, note that nothing is innocent. They decry the vast range of knowledge that it excludes, including those that center on issues of power and inequality such as emancipatory, feminist, and worker education. Paying attention to who holds knowledge, what knowledge carries weight, and what interests are served by particular forms of knowledge are important tools in struggles for social justice.

The chapters in this issue each grapple with some aspect of the rich and contested relationships between academic research and educational practice. The authors ask a range of questions including: What communities and experiences get included in, or excluded from, research? Whose knowledge is valued? How can those of us in the academy create and preserve space for diverse perspectives? How do issues of power manifest in attempts to build bridges beyond the ivory tower? Each chapter offers discussion of one facet of partnerships between communities and institutions of higher education. The chapters outline both the resulting challenges that arise and some strategies that were devised to address them. Throughout, the authors reflect on how such collaborations could be stronger and more effective.

New Directions for Adult and Continuing Education • DOI: 10.1002/ace

We hope that this issue offers examples that will deepen our understanding of the possibilities of democratic practice within various facets of adult education, but also examples that will heighten recognition of the dilemmas and contradictions that arise when we try to work across differences in privilege. We hope that this issue encourages readers to find ways to link politics, experiences, and academic knowledges—and ways to foreground understandings that are routinely sidelined. We anticipate that the examples outlined in these chapters will inspire you to develop partnerships that are mutually enriching and that build on the unique strengths and resources of each partner. Most of all we hope that this issue of *New Directions* will support you in continuing to reflect on the implications and challenges of working at the intersections and edges of the academy and community.

References

Allman, P. (1999). *Revolutionary social transformation: Democratic hopes, political possibilities and critical education.* Westport, CT: Bergin & Garvey.

Antone, E., Gamlin, P., & Provost-Turchetti, L. (2003). *Literacy and learning: Acknowledging aboriginal holistic approaches to learning in relation to "best practices" literacy training programs.* Retrieved from http://www.nald.ca/library/research/aboriglt/finlrprt/cover.htm

Arvast, A. (2006). From community to commodity college: Globalization, neoliberalism and the new Ontario college curricula. *Canadian Journal of Educational Administration and Policy, 50,* 1–21.

Balanoff, H., & Chambers, C. (2005). Do my literacies count as literacy: An inquiry into Inuinnaqtun literacies in the Canadian north. *Literacies, 6,* 18–20.

Bannerji, H. (2005). Building from Marx: Reflections on class and race. *Social Justice, 32*(4), 144–160.

Bathmaker, A.-M. (2007). The impact of Skills for Life on adult basic skills in England: How should we interpret trends in participation and achievement? *International Journal of Lifelong Education, 26*(3), 295–313.

Battell, E., Gesser, L., Rose, J., Sawyer, J., & Twiss, D. (2004). *Hardwired for hope: Effective ABE/literacy instructors.* Duncan, British Columbia, Canada: Malaspina University College.

Beach, D. (2003). A problem of validity in education research. *Qualitative Inquiry, 9*(6), 859–873. doi:10.1177/1077800403254807

Belzer, A., & St. Clair, R. (2005). Back to the future: Implications of the neopositivist research agenda for adult basic education. *Teachers College Record, 107*(6), 1393–1411. doi:10.1111/j.1467-9620.2005.00517.x

Campbell, P. (2003). *From coast to coast: A thematic summary of Canadian adult literacy research.* Ottawa, Ontario, Canada: National Literacy Secretariat.

Castro-Gómez, S. (2007). The missing chapter of empire: Postmodern reorganization of coloniality and post-Fordist capitalism. *Cultural Studies, 21*(2), 428–448. doi:10.1080/09502380601162639

Crooks, S., Davies, P., Gardner, A., Grieve, K., Mollins, T., Niks, M., . . . Wright, B. (2008). *Connecting the dots: Accountability in adult literacy—Voices from the field.* Montreal, Quebec, Canada: Centre for Literacy of Quebec.

Cussó, R., & D'Amico, S. (2005). From development comparatism to globalization comparativism: Towards more normative international education statistics. *Comparative Education, 41*(2), 199–216. doi:10.1080/03050060500037012

Darville, R. (2003). Making connections. *Literacies, 1,* 3–4.

Fejes, A., & Nicoll, K. (Eds.). (2008). *Foucault and lifelong learning: Governing the subject.* New York, NY: Routledge.

Fendler, L. (1998). What is it impossible to think? A genealogy of the educated subject. In T. S. Popkewitz & M. Brennan (Eds.), *Foucault's challenge: Discourse, knowledge, and power in education* (pp. 39–63). New York, NY: Teachers College Press.

Gomez, S. V. (2000). The collective that didn't quite collect: Reflections on the IALS. *International Review of Education, 46*(5), 419–431.

Grieve, K. (2003). *Supporting learning, supporting change: Developing an approach to helping learners build self-awareness and self-direction.* Toronto, Ontario, Canada: Ontario Literacy Coalition.

Hamilton, M. (2001). Privileged literacies: Policy, institutional process and the life of the IALS. *Language and Education, 15*(2–3), 178–196. doi:10.1080/09500780108666809

Hamilton, M. (2012). The effects of the literacy policy environment on local sites of learning. *Language and Education, 26*(2), 169–182. doi:10.1080/09500782.2011.642882

Hamilton, M., & Barton, D. (2000). The International Adult Literacy Survey: What does it really measure? *International Review of Education, 46*(5), 377–389.

Hamilton, M., & Tett, L. (2012). More powerful literacies: The policy context. In L. Tett, M. Hamilton, & J. Crowther (Eds.), *More powerful literacies* (pp. 31–57). Leicester, England: NIACE.

Hautecoeur, J. P. (1997). A political review of international literacy meetings in industrialized countries, 1981–1994. *International Review of Education, 43*(2–3), 135–158.

Hautecoeur, J. P. (2000). Literacy in the age of information: Knowledge, power or domination? *International Review of Education, 46*(5), 357–365. doi:10.1023/A:1004129812751

Hayes, B. (2009). From community development and partnerships to accountability: The case of the National Literacy Secretariat. *Literacies, 9,* 19–22.

Hernandez-Zamora, G. (2010). *Decolonizing literacy: Mexican lives in the era of global capitalism.* Bristol, England: Multilingual Matters.

Hillier, Y. (2009). The changing faces of adult literacy, language and numeracy: Literacy policy and implementation in the UK. *Compare: A Journal of Comparative and International Education, 39*(4), 535–550. doi:10.1080/03057920902833412

Horsman, J. (1999). *Too scared to learn: Women, violence and education.* Toronto, Ontario, Canada: McGilligan Books.

Horsman, J., & Norton, M. (1999). *A framework to encourage and support practitioner involvement in adult literacy research in practice in Canada.* Ottawa, Ontario, Canada: National Literacy Secretariat.

Horsman, J., & Woodrow, H. (Eds.). (2006). *Focused on practice: A framework for adult literacy research in Canada.* Vancouver, British Columbia, Canada: Literacy BC.

Jackson, N. S. (2005). Adult literacy policy: Mind the gap. In N. Bascia, A. Cumming, A. Datnow, K. Leithwood, & D. Livingstone (Eds.), *International handbook of educational policy* (pp. 763–778). Dordrecht, The Netherlands: Springer.

Kirsch, I. S., Jungeblut, A., Jenkins, L., & Kolstad, A. (2002). *Adult literacy in America: A first look at the findings of the National Adult Literacy Survey* (3rd ed.). Washington, DC: National Center for Education Statistics.

Lather, P. (2004). This IS your father's paradigm: Government intrusion and the case of qualitative research in education. *Qualitative Inquiry, 10*(1), 15–34. doi:10.1177/1077800403256154

LoBianco, J., & Wickert, R. (Eds.). (2001). *Australian policy activism in language and literacy.* Melbourne, Australia: Language Australia.

Manesse, D. (2000). Remarques critiques à propos de l'enquête internationale sur la litteratie [Critical Remarks Regarding the International Adult Literacy Survey]. *International Review of Education, 46*(5), 407–417.

Merrifield, J. (1997). *Life at the margins: Literacy, language, and technology in everyday life.* New York, NY: Teachers College Press.

Mignolo, W. D. (2013). Geopolitics of sensing and knowing: On (de)coloniality, border thinking, and epistemic disobedience. *Confero, 1*(1), 129–150. doi:10.3384/confero.2001-4562.13v1i1129

Myers, K., & de Broucker, P. (2006). *Too many left behind: Canada's adult education and training system*. Ottawa, Ontario, Canada: Canadian Policy Research Networks.

National Literacy Secretariat. (1996). *Working in concert: Federal, provincial and territorial actions in support of literacy in Canada*. Ottawa, Ontario, Canada: Author.

National Literacy Secretariat. (1998). *Enhancing literacy research in Canada*. Ottawa, Ontario, Canada: Author.

Ng, R., & Shan, H. (2010). Lifelong learning as ideological practice: An analysis from the perspective of immigrant women in Canada. *International Journal of Lifelong Education, 29*, 169–184.

Niks, M., Allen, D., Davies, P., McRae, D., & Nonesuch, K. (2003). *Dancing in the dark. How do adults with little formal education learn? How do literacy practitioners do collaborative research?* Duncan, British Columbia, Canada: Malaspina University College.

Norton, M. (Ed.). (2004). *Violence and learning: Taking action*. Calgary, Alberta, Canada: Literacy Alberta.

Norton, M., & Malicky, G. (Eds.). (2000). *Learning about participatory approaches in adult literacy education: Six research in practice studies*. Edmonton, Alberta, Canada: Learning at the Centre Press.

Norton, M., & Woodrow, H. (2001). *Looking back, looking in: Reports from "Bearing blossoms . . . sowing seeds."* Ottawa, Ontario, Canada: National Literacy Secretariat.

Ntiri, D. (2009). Framing the literacy issue: Correcting educational misrepresentations in U.S. society. *The Western Journal of Black Studies, 33*(4), 231–239.

OECD & Statistics Canada. (2000). *Literacy in the information age: Final report of the Adult Literacy Survey*. Paris, France: Organization for Economic Cooperation and Development (OECD). Retrieved from www.oecd.org/dataoecd/48/4/41529765.pdf

Peters, M. A., Besley, A. C., Olssen, M., Maurer, S., & Weber, S. (Eds.). (2009). *Governmentality studies in education*. Rotterdam, The Netherlands: Sense Publishers.

Popkewitz, T. S. (2012). The sociology of education as the history of the present: Fabrication, difference and abjection. *Discourse: Studies in the Cultural Politics of Education, 34*(3), 439–456. doi:10.1080/01596306.2012.717195

Quigley, B. A., Folinsbee, S., & Kraglund-Gauthier, W. (2006). *State of the field report: Adult literacy*. Antigonish, Nova Scotia, Canada: St Francis Xavier University.

Quigley, B. A., & Norton, M. (2002). *"It simply makes us better." Learning from literacy research in practice networks: A resource for literacy research in practice in Canada*. Edmonton, Alberta, Canada: Learning at the Centre Press.

Quijano, A. (2000). Coloniality of power, Eurocentrism, and Latin America. *Nepantla: Views from the South, 1*(3), 533–580.

Silver, J., Klyne, D., & Simard, F. (2003). *Aboriginal learners in selected adult learning centres in Manitoba*. Winnipeg, Manitoba, Canada: Canadian Centre for Policy Alternatives.

Smythe, S. (2011, June). *Certification for what? Practitioner perspectives on the changing landscape of adult literacy education*. Paper presented at the 52nd National Conference of the Adult Education Research Conference (AERC) & the 30th Conference of the Canadian Association for the Study of Adult Education (CASAE) Joint Meeting, Toronto, Ontario, Canada.

St. Clair, R. (2007). Approaching Canadian adult literacy research as a community of practice: Implications and possibilities. *Canadian Journal for the Study of Adult Education, 20*(1) 50–67.

Street, B. (2003). What's "new" in New Literacy Studies? Critical approaches to literacy in theory and practice. *Current Issues in Comparative Education, 5*(2), 77–91.

Tikly, L. (2009). Education and the new imperialism. In R. S. Coloma (Ed.), *Postcolonial challenges in education* (pp. 23–45). New York, NY: Peter Lang.

Trumpener, B. (1997). *Gimme shelter! A resource for literacy and homelessness work*. Retrieved from http://www.nald.ca/library/learning/homeless/lithome.htm

Tusting, K. (2012). Learning accountability literacies in educational workplaces: Situated learning and processes of commodification. *Language and Education, 26*(2), 121–138. doi:10.1080/09500782.2011.642879

Veeman, N., Ward, A., & Walker, K. (2006). *Valuing literacy in Canada: Rhetoric or reality?* Edmonton, Alberta, Canada: Detselig.

Woodrow, H. (2006). The state of the field. In J. Horsman & H. Woodrow (Eds.), *Focused on practice: A framework for adult literacy research in Canada* (pp. 21–31). Vancouver, British Columbia, Canada: Literacy BC.

Wrigley, H. S. (2005). The new school Canada: A comprehensive approach. *The National Youth Literacy Demonstration Project*. Vancouver, British Columbia, Canada: Literacy BC.

TANNIS ATKINSON worked as an educator and plain language editor for many years before becoming a doctoral student at the Ontario Institute for Studies in Education, University of Toronto, Canada.

2

This chapter presents one faculty member's narrative in which academic research, teaching, advising, and mentoring coalesced into an activist agenda for transformative learning and social justice.

Decentering and Recentering the Ivory Tower: The Insights and Musings of an Interloper

Juanita Johnson-Bailey

As adult educators who are professors in our educational discipline, we labor and struggle in our ivory tower of higher education, all the while attempting to create change by making our environment more inclusive in its representation and its practice. We proceed in this way because a primary tenet for adult educators is to empower adults and to provide an education that enhances lives (Cunningham, 1988). During my 20 years in the academy, I have attempted, like many adult education professors, to decenter my workplace, embracing the belief as set forth by Derrida (1978) in his essay, "Structure, Sign, and Play in the Discourse of the Human Sciences," that the center is not a fixed locus but one of function. From that perspective, decentering is an undertaking that I've focused on my entire career, even before I knew that there was a name for it. Decentering, from my perspective, as a Black woman academic, is most important to me since I often exist literally and figuratively as an outsider, an interloper, in this metaphoric ivory tower.

Before I can explain my outlook on decentering, I must problematize my position in academia. How do I write about changing this workplace in which I exist on the periphery? It is not that I haven't tried to be a full-fledged member, but it's a space that I've had a hard time occupying (Johnson-Bailey & Cervero, 2008).

For me, the ivory tower is a psychological space as well as a physical space where so many things happen from time to time that let me know that I am not really welcome in the physical space, and this impacts my ability to occupy the psychological space of being a professor. My favorite example of

NEW DIRECTIONS FOR ADULT AND CONTINUING EDUCATION, no. 139, Fall 2013 © 2013 Wiley Periodicals, Inc.
Published online in Wiley Online Library (wileyonlinelibrary.com) • DOI: 10.1002/ace.20060

how I am often pushed out of the figurative ivory tower occurred when I was leaving my office building with my laptop and a police officer stopped me to ask me where I was going with that laptop, assuming it wasn't mine. Fortunately, one of my students was in the parking lot. She waved, explaining I was her professor. Incidents exactly like this have happened to others of my African American colleagues, who can attest to what must appear a seemingly bizarre claim.

Occurrences like the parking lot incident initially shook me to my core. After all, being a professor was a lifelong dream. But upon critical reflection (Brookfield, 1995), I have learned to see such times as fortunate, and I've been able to be grateful for such clashes. Previously, I would have asked, "Why is this happening to me?" Now instead I ask, "Why is this happening for me?" I know that on some level the dilemma hides a lesson, a teachable moment, and an opportunity to grow.

I carry the knowledge that being an insider/outsider in the academy is a real gift. Seeing myself as an interloper keeps my perspectives charged. My standpoint as an outsider was bequeathed to me by a long line of people who didn't even know that the academy existed. And when my ancestors did know about the academy, they knew that they didn't have access to it. I was raised by these rebels to see the world as a classroom. For me the classroom is every-thing and everywhere and can transpire even in the nontraditional spaces occupied by a group of students and a teacher. Here is an example:

I had struggled so hard to try to get a concept across to students in my multicultural studies class: the universality of gender. The students, mostly African Americans, kept saying, "We get race." And while they did understand the concept of race and how racism worked, they could not grasp the inter-section of race and gender. Nor could they accept that gender and its opera-tionalized counterpart, sexism, was an enduring and more pervasive cog in the malevolent machine of oppressive "isms." I needed my students to see the intersection of gender and race and to understand how the powerful force of sexism could trump race and furthermore direct and determine the lives of women, historically and contemporarily. But as fate would have it, the oppor-tunity presented itself in 2000 in the Southern African country of Zimbabwe. A colleague, Dr. Talmadge Guy, and I were on our first study abroad. We had a serious problem. The Zimbabwe military intervened as we were attempting to cross the border into Botswana. As I was trying to explain to a solider that we were not trying to cheat them out of monies for fees charged to cross the border, he said, "Hush woman." An official then proceeded to talk to Dr. Guy. While the bureaucrat talked to Dr. Guy and the soldiers held AK 47s on me and a group of 11 women students, I leaned over to the students who had argued with me about the universality of gender. And I said, "So what color are the men with the guns?" And one of them said, "They are all Black." To which I responded, "Do you understand the universality of gender and sexism now?"

In part, recognizing this dilemma as a teachable moment is a gift that is directly connected to my interloper's existence. And so I am happy to accept

New Directions for Adult and Continuing Education • DOI: 10.1002/ace

the bitter parts, the many occasions when I am not recognized as a faculty member, or I am questioned about my competence as a faculty member, as a price worth paying for the sweet thrill and stimulating parts that enable and allow me to perch on the teachable ledge.

So like so many adult educators who try to make change in our setting, to make space (Sheared, 1994), we are not attempting to overthrow or to destroy our environment by decentering. We are trying to recenter academia, in part by embodying the change.

Do you remember why you became a teacher/educator/practitioner? I do. It drives and determines what I do each and every day. And here's the back story. It's part of my teaching philosophy statement that I distribute to the students in my reflective practice class:

> My first day of kindergarten was also my first day as a teacher. Every day I would run the two blocks home to teach my grandmother my lessons for the day. I was determined that she would learn to sign her name S.A.R.A.H. and not X. Although she was my first pupil, she was also one of my first and best teachers. Mama Sarah did not learn to write her name, but she did learn to recognize it in my kindergartner's scrawl. More important for me was that she encouraged my learning and teaching and engendered in me a joy for this dynamic process—a process that is urgent and essential.

Nothing makes me happier, more anxious, more energetic, or uncertain than teaching. Teaching is an evolving ever-changing process. For teaching is a three-way exchange and both the learners and the context will impact the way that the class proceeds. Therefore, no class that I teach is ever the same. I find this preparation sometimes exhausting, but it's such an exciting and synergistic way to live. Despite my need to wrap my curriculum around my students (Sealey-Ruiz, 2007), there are nonnegotiable standards: My courses are writing- and reading-intensive. Invariably nothing makes a student think more than reading challenging materials and being required to critically react to the new information. Additionally, needs assessment is essential to making the course responsive and fulfilling to my students as we are obligated to find out what our students need.

Furthermore, by letting my students know that I am receptive to their needs, a sense of reciprocity is established. Inevitably the canon must be center stage in the classroom, but how we approach is not predetermined. And "troubling" the assignments by posing critical questions to the readings is one certain way to expand the discussion. What's more, since I believe that good teaching is about an exchange, I do my best to teach my students. In return, my students have never failed to teach me.

And so in recentering the ivory tower, teaching is the lifeline, the connection, the conduit for change and student empowerment. It is incumbent upon us as agents of change, as champions for social justice, to leave our classrooms, whether they are our virtual ones or face-to-face, better than we found them. It is essential that we work toward empowering our students, our co-learners. And teaching is not an act or practice that commences when you walk into the classroom and ends when you exit.

To illustrate this, I offer you the story of Lena and Amille, two students that are part of a 2004 research study, *Hitting and Climbing the Proverbial Wall: Participation and Retention Issues for Black Graduate Women* (Johnson-Bailey, 2004). The women endured several unusual difficulties while attempting to enroll in graduate school. In this research study, Lena, a 48-year-old housing administrator, was stalled in her application process since the graduate coordinator related to her that he did not feel that she was "graduate school material." However, the university official did not explain his assessment to Lena, leaving her overwhelmed in self-doubt and assuming that the seasoned credential professor and graduate coordinator knew best. It would be 18 years before she found the fortitude and confidence to question his speedy and harsh assessment, driven by a developing sense of self that she established by mastering and outgrowing her uncertainty. When Lena finally applied to a different college at the same university, she was accepted; has completed both her master's and doctoral degrees; and has gone on to receive national recognition for a program that she designed to solicit community involvement for low-income women.

Another similarly situated student, Amille, a 44-year-old hospital administrator, recalled that she went to visit a prospective graduate program to get an application. However, the department head, who was also the graduate coordinator, refused to give her any materials when he discovered that she intended to be a part-time graduate student. In his words, she was not a serious student because she intended to continue working full-time and pursue school part-time. Amille did not get a degree from that communications graduate program, but she did get an education from that university; and she now holds a professorship at a research university. Even though both of these women have gone on to make important contributions, despite the system, what happens to the countless Lenas and Amilles who don't persist?

Women have been returning to school in record numbers since 1970 and currently represent 56% of the U.S. college population (NCES, 2012). So why do women college students still describe higher education as a chilly climate? In the words of an esteemed scholar, Marvin Gaye, "It makes me wanna holler, and throw up both my hands!" (Gaye & Nyx, 1971, track 9). And, as Gaye suggests in another song, it makes me wonder, "What's going on?" (Cleveland, Benson, & Gaye, 1971, track 1).

With higher education portrayed as being the democratic place of free thinkers and liberals, we are left to ask, do things change once our students gain entry? Does it matter if they are working class, nontraditional, first-generation, Black, White, Latina, gay, straight? I wish the answer were yes. But the answer is, it shouldn't matter but in some instances it does. Aren't we a bastion of inclusivity? Again, I wish the answer were yes. But in my experience, it's, "We're trying. We're putting up a good fight."

New Directions for Adult and Continuing Education • DOI: 10.1002/ace

In this changing world, where demographics are rapidly shifting and neighbors can be across the street or across the world, we as educators know that it is imperative to make our practices inclusive because research is definitive about the ways in which students are impacted by what happens in the schooling environment. Disenfranchised students—students of color, gay students—routinely experience higher education as an insensitive or a competitively hostile environment, which causes psychological distress that can result in withdrawal, feelings of loneliness, self-doubt, and lowered self-concept. Such factors significantly affect student satisfaction (Nettles & Millett, 2006; Swim, Hyers, Cohen, Fitzgerald, & Bylsma, 2003). A compounding dilemma results because student satisfaction has been shown to influence the performance and completion rate for these same students. Additionally, lack of social integration, infrequent participation in campus organizations and activities, and limited interaction with peers and faculty have more of an impact on the grade point averages of these disenfranchised students (Nettles, 1988). Inevitably such issues as isolation, loneliness, self-doubt, and lowered self-concept have had a negative effect on progression rates for students. So for these students, interactions with faculty members can positively affect development and advancement with increased competence and improved self-confidence.

As educators, we are on the front lines in attempting to make education liberating and empowering. Our schools reflect our society. We work and learn side by side and yet we lack knowledge about those who are different. And so this major system that we are a part of, higher education, which could sponsor change, continues to reproduce existing systems of power, and functions to maintain the status quo. Our Western society is based on a hierarchical system where privilege is usually accorded along existing lines of established rights and entitlement. Many variables drive our society. The powerful systems of disenfranchisement abound: sexism, heterosexism, ageism, classism, and racism. The context of our multicultural world is varied and complicated by these powerful systems that carry with them a set of beliefs. These systems accompany our students into their classrooms. Add to that the fact that what is accepted as knowledge is political and the dilemma is apparent.

In the academy, whether we participate as students, instructors, or planners, we bring the historical weight of our positionalities with us. It matters little whether we intentionally trade on or naively try to discard the privileges, the deficits, or the standpoints of our statuses. Such ranks, authorizations, honors, suspicions, and stereotypes cannot be cast aside. They are accrued in society's invisible socially ordered banking system of trading and bartering according to designated rankings. If we are to change and function more proficiently, then we must acknowledge and manage the uninvited specters that haunt us in the United States. Culturally inclusive pedagogy is tailored to fit the needs and abilities of its students (Sealey-Ruiz, 2007).

New Directions for Adult and Continuing Education • DOI: 10.1002/ace

As teachers we must be aware that humans are social beings and that culture provides a basis to explain how groups make sense of shared values, attitudes, beliefs, and behaviors. I want to suggest that we can be more effective as educators if we attend to the teaching/learning transaction. First, we must begin by closely examining ourselves and our practices. Being tuned into culture in your classroom positively affects the psychological, social, and academic environment. If the culture of the teacher is to become part of the consciousness of the student, then the culture of the student must be in the consciousness of the teacher. Teaching is not a unidirectional process.

While the science, the practice, and the art of teaching are important, another important part of the equation is how we teach the subject. And the resulting inclusive pedagogy is one of the keys to recentering our educational product and thereby maximizing our students' human potential.

Quite often we as teachers focus only on what is to be learned. Depending on your academic discipline, it may be the most up-to-date studies in sociology, what the academic journals are saying about research methods, or new ways of preparing preservice teachers. There is no area where knowledge remains stagnant, not even the classics, as new information is found about the authors or old manuscripts are reexamined and questioned and missing manuscripts are discovered. Quite often I hear from colleagues that they understand how I might apply the idea of an inclusive, culturally responsive pedagogy to sociology or social work or teacher education, but not the area in which they teach. Well, there are no exceptions. One can design a culturally responsive pedagogy regardless of subject matter (Guy, 1999; Tisdell, 1995).

What professors must understand is that each curriculum has a culture, and that certain types of students may not understand or have sufficient cultural capital to navigate this new foreign culture. This idea resonates with Huo and Molina's scholarship on subgroups (2006). They set forth that subgroup cultures have to be attended to in the educational arena. And it is imperative to the teaching/learning process that subgroup identities be acknowledged.

Studies done by teachers who were action researchers in their own practices found that just telling the students about the achievements of the "other" inspired and facilitated the work of the students who looked like the "others," and it did not negatively impact the performance of students in the majority group.

According to Tisdell (1995), it is best and most effective if we choose not only the additive method but the transformative method in creating our inclusive pedagogies. By emphasizing inclusion, we are affirming that we want all students to participate in our classes and we know that for some groups who are characteristically silent or silenced this may involve a conscious effort on our part to make space. Directly connected to the issue of inclusion are the concepts of transformation and empowerment, which does not connote for us the process of self-actualization often discussed in the literature, but instead means that the student has a sense of belongingness and equity as a full member of the class collective. Again, working toward an environment where the student is empowered involves managing classroom dynamics to ensure that student–student, teacher–student, and curriculum–class exchanges are positive and constructive. It is our goal to try to ensure that students experience our classrooms as safe spaces where they can openly express their doubts, confront the unknown, and carve out and claim their own intellectual space, constructing a participatory educational environment that is grounded in respect.

Finally, it is important to always remember that an ideal teaching environment is built on reciprocity. Our students bring a wealth of experience and knowledge from their varying histories, contexts, geographies, and biographies. It is our responsibility to recognize, highlight, and honor their contributions. We must acknowledge that there are no ultimate truths or validity to the values that Eurocentric ideals imply; more important, we must manifest this knowledge within our classrooms.

It is our "ethical" responsibility as feminists, antiracists, supporters of social justice, people who speak the diversity speak and walk the diversity walk to go beyond words, to move beyond the "diversity day" or "diversity month" or the "diversity mission." We must continue to question how we are defining inclusion. And we must ask, "Is everyone benefiting in real material ways from our practices? Are we making change? How are we accountable?"

As a woman of color teaching in an adult education graduate program and researching and writing about race and gender, I can easily lose sight of my own privilege: I have a terminal degree; I am tenured; I am able-bodied; I am a married heterosexual; I am middle-class. While my research critiques the hegemonic relations between the powerful and the powerless, and despite the overall disenfranchisement of Black women, I generally have a comfortable existence. To reconcile my academic place of comfort with my real world position, I frequently revisit the variances of my background, a cultural therapy exercise that assesses how culture affects teaching/learning (Banks, 1994). I have to ask myself if my actions match my rhetoric.

Final Thoughts

Teaching, advising, and mentoring are ways in which we as academics work to decenter and recenter our academy. In particular, the practice and art of teaching requires us to perform a spectacular juggling act if we want to develop and maintain an inclusive pedagogy and pedagogical style. In spite of this, from what I know adult educators do it all quite well.

There are five guiding rules that help me with decentering and recentering this academic landscape:

1.   Always ask if you are part of the solution or the problem.
2.   Be flexible, responsive, and steadfast.

3. Remember, no matter how far one travels, one never reaches a final destination of establishing a place that is safe and fair.
4. Learn, grow, and adjust because it's a continuous process for both the student and the faculty member.
5. It's hard work; it never gets easier; but it is effort that is worth the endeavor.

If you accept nothing else of what I have to offer, take note of this: As adult educators, we are doing important, essential work, providing a knowledge base and empowerment tools that help students. It is noble work that contributes to the struggle for societal equality and is an important mission.

Less than 50 years ago, higher education looked different. The membership was restricted by gender, race and class, national origin, and physical ability. Now the once fortified gateway to higher education is more open and the academic landscape is more reflective of U.S. society; however, we have not reached nirvana. As scholars and educators, our actions make a difference. We have to strive to recenter our academic workplace, making it an effective and welcoming environment that provides equal access and opportunity to all students and faculty who enter the gates.

And it is challenging for students and teachers alike to see their assumptions and to critically examine what they regard as their universal truths (Takacs, 2002), since as humans we are inevitably mired in seeking out data to support what we already know. It can become an exercise in relativism and futility (Moser, 2008), with positional stances being simultaneously significant and insignificant, depending on the situation and/or the discourse. By existing in this way, we are more vulnerable, but we are practicing from our souls, modeling how to take risks and be open to new ideas, welcoming disparate voices.

Using such an approach has changed our field. To illustrate this point, I end with the following story:

In 2012 as we celebrate the 20th anniversary of the African Diaspora Pre-Conference, it's important to remember that there have been years when the African Diaspora Pre-Conference host sites questioned the need to have the pre-conference as a part of it. On two occasions host universities insisted that holding such a pre-conference was an example of "reverse discrimination." In other years the pre-conference was relegated to back-of-the-bus locations, away from the main conference.

Then after years of struggle, when the African Diaspora found itself entrenched as an acceptable part of African Diaspora Pre-Conference history, its executive committee discovered the Lesbian, Gay, Bisexual, Transsexual, and Questioning Pre-Conference was being told by a host site committee that they were unwelcome. Upon inquiring the African Diaspora executive committee was told, "We'll take the African Diaspora Pre-Conference, but we don't want the LGBTQ Pre-Conference." And the response from the African Diaspora Pre-Conference was immediate, "That means you don't want us. You

New Directions for Adult and Continuing Education • DOI: 10.1002/ace

don't take them; you don't have us. That's the way it works." The African Diaspora executive committee had learned important lessons from their experiences—the overt challenges and instances of benign neglect—and held the knowledge that their origins were inclusive and that one of their primary purposes was bringing in members of the adult education community who had been primarily unrepresented and voiceless.

This little-known story is a tale of how the ivory tower of adult education was transformed through struggle and coalitions between disenfranchised communities who carried an understanding that we are all connected. In this decentering and recentering of our academic environment, we have been made all the better.

References

Banks, J. A. (1994). *An introduction to multicultural education*. Needham Heights, MA: Allyn & Bacon.

Brookfield, S. D. (1995). *Becoming a critically reflective teacher*. San Francisco, CA: Jossey-Bass.

Cleveland, A., Benson, R., & Gaye, M. (1971). What's going on [Recording by M. Gaye]. On *What's going on* [Audio CD]. Detroit, MI: Motown.

Cunningham, P. M. (1988). The adult educator and social responsibility. In R. G. Brockett (Ed.), *Ethical issues in adult education* (pp. 133–145). New York, NY: Teachers College Press.

Derrida, J. (1978). *Writing and difference*. Chicago, IL: University of Chicago Press.

Gaye, M., & Nyx, J., Jr. (1971). Inner city blues (Make me wanna holler) [Recording by M. Gaye]. On *What's going on* [Audio CD]. Detroit, MI: Motown.

Guy, T. C. (1999). Culture as context for adult education: The need for culturally relevant adult education. In T. C. Guy (Ed.), *New Directions for Adult and Continuing Education: No. 82. Providing culturally relevant adult education: A challenge for the twenty-first century* (pp. 5–18). San Francisco, CA: Jossey-Bass.

Huo, Y. J., & Molina, L. E. (2006). Is pluralism a viable model of diversity? The benefits and limits of subgroup respect. *Group Processes & Intergroup Relations, 9*(3), 359–376.

Johnson-Bailey, J. (2004). Hitting and climbing the proverbial wall: Participation and retention issues for Black graduate women. *Race, Ethnicity, & Education, 7*(4), 331–349.

Johnson-Bailey, J., & Cervero, R. M. (2008). Different worlds & divergent paths: Academic careers defined by race and gender. *Harvard Educational Review, 78*(2), 311–332.

Moser, S. (2008). Personality: A new positionality. *AREA, 40*(3), 383–392.

National Center for Education Statistics (NCES). (2012). *Digest of Education Statistics, 2011.* Washington, DC: U.S. Department of Education.

Nettles, M. T. (Ed.). (1988). *Toward Black undergraduate student equality in American higher education*. Westport, CT: Greenwood Press.

Nettles, M. T., & Millett, C. M. (2006). *Three magic letters: Getting to Ph.D.* Baltimore, MD: Johns Hopkins University Press.

Sealey-Ruiz, Y. (2007). Wrapping the curriculum around their lives: Using a culturally relevant curriculum with African American adult women. *Adult Education Quarterly, 58*(1), 44–60.

Sheared, V. (1994). Giving voice: An inclusive model of instruction: A womanist perspective. In E. Hayes & S. A. J. Colin, III (Eds.), *Confronting racism and sexism* (pp. 27–38). San Francisco, CA: Jossey-Bass.

Swim, J., Hyers, L., Cohen, L., Fitzgerald, D., & Bylsma, W. (2003). African American col-
lege students' experiences with everyday racism. *Journal of Black Psychology, 29*(1),
38–67.
Takacs, D. (2002). Positionality, epistemology, and social justice in the classroom. *Social
Justice, 29*(4), 168–181.
Tisdell, E. J. (1995). *Creating inclusive adult learning environments: Insights from multicultural
education and feminist pedagogy* (Information Series No. 361). Columbus, OH: ERIC
Clearinghouse on Adult, Career, and Vocational Education.

JUANITA JOHNSON-BAILEY is a professor of adult education and women's studies.

3

This article traces the author's personal reflections on the complexity and contradictions inherent in working for social change. She describes her experiences of movement-based learning and organizing to end poverty in the United States, concluding that radical adult educators cannot afford to be based solely within the academy, divorced from spaces that rest on a love of learning for the purpose of liberation.

Decentering the Ivory Tower: A University of the Poor

Shivaani A. Selvaraj

On a wall in my home, I have a framed newspaper article that I found in my files from the *Patriot-News* in 1996 with a story titled "Homeless proclaim success, end Capitol protest" (Krebs, 1996). This was the lead story in the central Pennsylvanian daily newspaper's local and state section after the end of a 37-day protest that culminated with the governor conceding to a plan for a "Poor People's Embassy" in Harrisburg, Pennsylvania, that would track legislation, educate the public, and provide social services and housing to the low income (Gilbert, 2001). This ended up being yet another example of false promises made by politicians in response to confrontations from activists demanding responsibility for worsening conditions for low-income people. It also appeared to be a short-lived victory for the Philadelphia-based organization that had marched for a week from Philadelphia to Harrisburg and then camped in the rotunda of the state capitol. Seen in a wider context, this and several other audacious campaigns have altered the lives and paths of many and have contributed to the politicization and development of dozens of new leaders for social change. Further, this is a sliver of an important untold aspect of U.S. history—low-income people's organizing across racial divisions to end poverty in the United States (Baptist & Rehmann, 2011). I have had the opportunity to take part in this work at various moments alongside others, and it has been formative in my practice and inquiry into radical adult education. I now live in Harrisburg, Pennsylvania's state capital, where I work and study at the Harrisburg campus of Penn State University. This story is part of my reflections on my journey and the question of decentering the academy for activist-scholars.

NEW DIRECTIONS FOR ADULT AND CONTINUING EDUCATION, no. 139, Fall 2013 © 2013 Wiley Periodicals, Inc.
Published online in Wiley Online Library (wileyonlinelibrary.com) • DOI: 10.1002/ace.20061

25

A Narrative That Began Before Me

For the 2012 Adult Education Research Conference I was asked to speak on a plenary panel exploring the topic of "decentering the academy." I was drawn to share experiences from the antipoverty organizing and educating work I was a part of in Philadelphia. This work was bold and defiant. To this day, I feel like a stranger in most dominant institutions. For the majority of my adult years I have worked toward the transformation of society and it is the radical tradition within adult education that has appealed to me and drawn me into academic study. From this perspective, decentering the academy lies in prioritizing the advancement of a political agenda to make society freer and more equal through radical educational programs tied to action (Allman, 2010; Brookfield & Holst, 2011; Foley, 2001). In preparation for writing this chapter I had the insight that there has never been a time in my life that the academy has not been a presence, even if it was the site against which to rebel. This is a narrative that began before me. My Indian parents met while teaching at a university in India, after attending graduate schools in the United States and Canada. They agreed to immigrate to the United States, largely with the idea that I would have more educational opportunities if I was a U.S. citizen, and therefore more life opportunities. I was born 1 month after they arrived, the daughter of two Indian scientists. The Immigration and Nationality Act of 1965, which allowed their entry to the United States, replaced an earlier racist quota system with preferences based primarily on skills and family reunification (Takaki, 1989). The academy, as the engine of expert knowledge and a contributor to policy creation, has shaped my existence from the very start.

The first of my family born in the United States, I grew up in the Boston area, searching for language and ways to understand the contradictory existence of inequalities, injustices, and privilege, not to mention my feelings of anger, always with a critical eye toward the American dream. This quest has continually led me toward people and organizations engaged in work for social change. I first heard the phrase "movements begin with the telling of untold stories" circulating in the early 1990s among antipoverty activists in Philadelphia. I had just arrived there to attend the University of Pennsylvania, already skeptical about institutions and searching for political activity and expression that would challenge systems at their root. It was a striking time to be in Philadelphia—the visibility of poverty was overwhelming. This was just before neoliberal urban policies were put into place (Harvey, 2005; Sager, 2011), meant to literally sweep poverty out of sight. But in the early 1990s, poverty was in people's daily consciousness. The underground subway corridor in Center City was lined every night with hundreds of cardboard boxes where many people slept because the shelter system was full. A statistic that antipoverty activists broadcast was that there were about 30,000 abandoned houses and there were about 30,000 homeless people. The simple everyday activity of walking around my neighborhood took me back and forth between

New Directions for Adult and Continuing Education • DOI: 10.1002/ace

the elitism of Penn and the conditions faced by Philadelphia's most impoverished. I was driven to explore and understand these contradictions and rebel against Penn's self-congratulatory calls for service and sharing expertise to solve community problems. I joined a student organization that called for an end to band-aid solutions to poverty and collaborated with organizations that were led by low-income people. I had the rare experience of being mentored by homeless and formerly homeless leaders who taught me about being an intellectual and activist. Being situated in Philadelphia facilitated my exposure to such networks, ideas, and alternative practice. I learned to intentionally cultivate my perspectives and choose the activity I committed myself to carefully. This allowed me to negotiate, however uneasily, my presence within the institution with the antipoverty work that challenged the very elitism upon which Penn was founded.

During this time, I collaborated with people striving intellectually and practically to move beyond the pervasive logic of capitalism. In this context, I was exposed for the first time to disciplined, rigorous, collective, and self-directed study. I learned to read and analyze academic and other texts from the standpoint of the low income. This translated into concrete skills and awareness that helped me to distinguish between types of knowledge and to identify silences, gaps in analysis, and ruling ideologies. Within the student organization, we adopted a rather unforgiving critique of service providers and charities as "poverty pimps," who furthered their professions by managing poverty while reinforcing status quo social relations. Study emerging from our political struggles sought to understand the current world order from a historical and materialist perspective. In response to more immediate crises, the student group, which by then attracted young people from across the country, chose our activities in cooperation with the low-income-led organizations. The most significant of these activities involved researching federally owned abandoned properties, working with community-based lawyers, and organizing housing "takeovers." Prior to this we sometimes helped to set up tent cities on abandoned lots where homeless families might live for months. We would build relationships with the community, gather food donations, care for children, work security, get press attention, and participate in educational and strategy sessions. Then we took the houses and housed these families. In court and in the public sphere, we fought the federal government on moral as well as legal grounds. Though short-lived, housing takeovers allowed us to force confrontation and create a space of struggle, where we were able to imagine and practice a vision outside the logic of capitalism, and work collectively to expose the reality behind the American Dream. Sometimes we won houses for people. Sometimes the struggle was more symbolic; we worked with human rights lawyers to sue the United States for economic human rights violations. It was through these experiences that I learned about power, government priorities, cross-racial and cross-class learning and organizing. Building a social movement in the United States to end poverty has also been a way for me to resolve the heartbreak of my parents' immigration in search of opportunities.

New Directions for Adult and Continuing Education • DOI: 10.1002/ace

The Evolution of a University of the Poor

There is a long and deep history of radical education, critical consciousness creation, and movement-based learning outside the university structure. Others have detailed various aspects of this history from the perspective of adult education (Jesson & Newman, 2004; Preskill & Brookfield, 2009). The organizing experience that grew in Philadelphia falls within this longer tradition. We looked to that history and models from around the globe to learn about the role of political education in social movement formation and the relationship of social movements to political party formation. Within U.S. history we drew on symbols and experiences that linger in people's memory and imagination, which can be channeled into motion today. Several aspects of the civil rights movement inspired our work, including the interracial Freedom Rides into the segregated South, the Citizenship Schools held at the Highlander Folk School, and the network of Freedom Schools of 1964 in Mississippi. Knowledge of these experiences directly contributed to specific strategies in later iterations of antipoverty work in order to bring attention to the growing problem of poverty in the United States, examine current issues collectively, and develop learning through leadership. As we worked on housing takeovers and other *projects of survival*, we also created opportunities to study power in Philadelphia, neoliberalism at the municipal and global levels, media and communications, among other topics. Finally, Martin Luther King, Jr.'s legacy was influential as a precursor to cross-racial organizing. Martin Luther King decried the gap between rich and poor and announced the Poor People's Campaign close to the time of his assassination when his attention moved toward antimilitarism and economic justice across racial lines (Cohen & Solomon, 1995). The work that I belonged to and that continues today across the country operates from the shared analysis that class continues to be relevant (Nesbit, 2005) and the polarization of wealth is the defining issue of today (Baptist & Rehmann, 2011).

The idea that poverty exists in the United States is not surprising today, but still the magnitude and diversity of poverty continues to be masked in mainstream media and discourse. How poverty is defined and by whom has implications for what solutions seem logical and possible. Who are the poor— are they the 99%, or will we limit discussion and attention to those living in extreme poverty who exist on less than one dollar per day? The mass media, serving as mass educator of adults, has tended to define poverty in narrow terms and to focus coverage of poverty in the United States on urban women of color, exacerbating divides across racial, gender, and geographic lines (Baptist, 2010; Macek, 2006). In 1994, I attended the Break the Media Blackout Conference on Penn's campus, organized by the same local collaboration between students and low-income-led organizations. This national gathering brought together other low-income-led organizations, artists, journalists, independent media makers, and people of faith. We discussed the policies of the Federal Communications Commission and histories of cross-racial antipoverty organizing in the United States that are not taught; we conducted a "reality tour" of Philadelphia; and because of the foresight of my friend and peer, Chris Caruso, we discussed the promise of the Internet. This conference was an early attempt at bringing together people operating in different sectors and raising awareness of the centrality of communications in antipoverty work. Conversations began here about the significance of independent media within movements regarding the necessity of defining the terms of debate and interrupting mainstream media's ability to equate people's sense of power with consumption. Instead, movement media held the potential to emphasize analysis, perspectives, and voices of people most adversely affected by economic policies, as well as stories about how this segment of society builds power through organizing.

Study and experience furthered our understanding of the interrelation of systems and institutional complexes. In 1996, welfare reform (the cutting back of welfare) passed, as did media reform (the further corporate consolidation of mainstream media). We saw changes as Philadelphia adopted neoliberal policies as the competition for global capital intensified among urban areas (Harvey, 2005; Smith, 2002). As people became impoverished and security nets were dismantled, gentrification increased and a beautified version of Philadelphia came to dominate the local media, replacing coverage of the increasing poverty and antipoverty organizing. A second Break the Media Blackout conference, held on Temple University's campus in 2002, focused equally on the state of the economy and antipoverty organizing around the United States, media literacy, political economy of the mass media, and independent media production (Themba-Nixon & Rubin, 2003). As the antipoverty work grew nationally, there was a real challenge of forging connections among people who have never thought of themselves in relation to each other. Two-month-long national *New Freedom* bus tours in 1998 and 2002 began in Philadelphia and stopped in more than 20 cities, towns, and rural areas. These tours provided a meeting point for organized groups to begin the hard work of breaking through racial stereotypes exacerbated by media portrayals. Exchanging stories with people in farming counties in Kansas, housing projects in Chicago, and migrant communities along the border in El Paso facilitated irreplaceable learning opportunities about similarities and differences in ways that people struggle and about the complexity of poverty across the United States. These national "reality tours" laid the groundwork for a "University of the Poor" made up of various schools and colleges from different sectors—social workers, artists, young people, religious leaders, and media professionals—to collectively study, share, and reflect on experiences and strategies emerging across the country. These were collaborations between low-income people's organizations and people in various professions developing educational components to accompany organizing efforts, created in the interests of low-income people.

New Directions for Adult and Continuing Education • DOI: 10.1002/ace

Strong in these experiences and the belief that a social movement in the United States is necessary, a small group of leaders organized a trip to visit Brazil's *Movimento dos Trabalhadores Sem Terra*. This movement of landless workers fighting for land reform and sustainable agriculture is 1.5 million strong and is known for its strategy of occupying and settling land. One of our goals of this exchange was to learn about their activities and systems for education and leadership development. We visited massive tent cities housing families and the communities that were settled after winning the land, where movement participants had built schools for children and farmed medicinal gardens in addition to traditional farming. We also stayed at the Popular University of Social Movements in São Paulo, built to accommodate movement members from different parts of the country. Curriculum is designed for different levels and purposes, including basic literacy, secondary education, various technical training, and the close reading and debate over political texts by Gramsci, Freire, Marx, Lenin, Luxembourg, and others. Inspired by this and other models for political education and popular universities, intensive "leadership schools" were (and continue to be) organized in the U.S. context to study and analyze current conditions and the histories behind them, share lessons and experiences from across the country, and develop leadership operating from shared understandings. Collective knowledge emerged from and in the interests of the lowest strata of society, in a process explicitly meant to unsettle the status quo. As a participant in these visionary projects for over a decade, I obtained a view of a rarely exposed side of the United States and cultivated a perspective that I have continued to explore.

Over time, specific organizations and networks have come and gone; some have lasted, though not currently under the name of University of the Poor. Many leaders from the earlier period and newer generations of leaders are working to construct knowledge about power as they work to build it. Ideas stemming from experiences in this period of my life continue to be resurrected, debated, and tested in new projects and institutions. The concept of the University of the Poor is likely to launch again in the near future. I went on to cofound the Media Mobilizing Project in 2005, an organization that incorporated some of these ideas and lessons from the use of independent media and communication technology in international social movements, and championed the necessity of an independent media infrastructure in social movement building (Berger, Funke, & Wolfson, 2011). Radical education within the organization is developed for a variety of audiences to examine historical, socioeconomic, and political trends, and the role of communication technology and media in organizing for a new society. Specialized media education consists of digital literacy, media literacy, and hard-skills trainings in audio or video production. Across several of the organizations that currently work together, there is a shared appreciation of the political nature of defining poverty and the ways that mainstream media fragments and isolates individuals and groups within society (Funke, Robe, & Wolfson, 2012).

New Directions for Adult and Continuing Education • DOI: 10.1002/ace

Returning to the Ivory Tower

After Media Mobilizing Project got off the ground, I returned to the university setting to attend a master's program in instructional technology. After years of experimenting with new technologies for educational and organizing purposes without any formal training, I was interested in building up concrete skills through sustained study. When I came to Penn State in 2010 to work as an instructional designer, I was not planning on entering graduate school again for a doctoral program, and I was not familiar with adult education as a field of study. This is not where I imagined myself landing, especially since my activist history in Philadelphia, which began in 1991, was in part borne from resisting the academy. I remember being surprised by the "mechanical nature" of the learning design process that I was taught in graduate school. The technical writing involved in drafting design documents, outlining learning objectives, and developing the corresponding assessment items seemed to have little in common with the years I spent designing education to change people's hearts and minds and ultimately, the world. Later, I became interested in critiques of technical rational processes and the debates surrounding the professionalization of the adult education field. Perhaps I entered these disciplines somewhat naively, but the theoretical debates gave me some insight into what strikes me as diminished curiosity and narrowness of vision within these professions. This has been in stark contrast to the commitment to thinking big and globally that has been the norm in my work for social change. I have also frequently encountered the attitude that the critical/radical traditions of social inquiry tend to be long on critique and short on solutions. These views can be misleading to newcomers in graduate study who may not be aware of the existence of organized radical education coupled with organized activity within the United States and elsewhere. Further, such opinions mask how many so-called solutions to social ills result in inadvertent consequences (Jackson, 1995; Murray, 2012; Rankin & Campbell, 2009). By default, most students' interests are shaped in part by the absence of information and substantive exposure. I do not mean this as a criticism of individual educators. Rather, this is an observation of how institutions mediate our daily lives within universities and interfere with even our best intentions.

I believe that it is imperative that adult education scholars develop comprehensive analysis that seeks to map oppression in the largest possible context, even if it seems grandiose. I am encouraged by critical research methods that do not take academic knowledge as the sole authority. It occurs to me that a simple and straightforward way to decenter the ivory tower is to act on the understanding that knowledge creation does not only originate within the academy. However, there is ultimately no place of innocence upon which to stand. All of us are implicated in perpetuating existing oppressive systems and social relations, within and outside the academy. There are those in the adult education field who are invested in questioning whether adult education is

New Directions for Adult and Continuing Education • DOI: 10.1002/ace

truly an agent for change, or rather an instrument in the service of status quo political and economic agendas (Mojab, 2009; Mott, 2006). Frontline workers within organized labor and grassroots organizations are also compromised in daily dealings. In 2006, I participated in a decision-making process to incorporate the organization I cofounded as a 501(c)3 nonprofit entity. While the organization continues the early commitment to economic justice across racial lines, nonprofit incorporation has necessarily opened the organization to new influences and trajectories. A necessary, intensified focus on fund-raising and organizational development threatens to shift the focus of day-to-day work activities. How the organization currently navigates federal guidelines and regulations as it implements federal funding to manage public computer centers and design and deliver digital literacy programs is the subject of my doctoral research.

My current place in the academy has allowed me to continue learning, reflecting, and engaging with the work in Philadelphia, now through the problematic position as a researcher. I notice how my voice is different in that space as questions are now more common than answers and conviction is no longer grounded in experience. I have only recently begun to feel that my academic endeavors may be of use to my friends and peers. Frequently, I have felt that sharing experiences from my past work is far more useful to those in the academy, mostly as a reminder that there are still those who believe in and work for social change and work for it on a daily basis. Knowledge creation in these contexts, which may not be considered legitimate by those in the ivory tower, generates critical analysis to guide action for change versus descriptive critique (Ebert, 1996) of various positions within academic literature. The history of the housing takeovers is a story from the margins, which Martin (2006) argues is a dangerous and precarious place. This is a particular slice of history within the United States that faces the threat of disappearance, but has the potential to threaten the status quo. History told through a critical lens contextualizes past campaigns and sets the foundation to understand current conditions and the role and form of resistance today. These "untold stories," past and present, are meant to raise new questions about the economy, society, and culture. They also help motivate people to act using theories, practices, and tools that are appropriate to their historic moment. Radical adult educators cannot afford to base themselves solely within the academy, divorced from spaces that rest on a love of learning for the purpose of liberation. What could adult education look like if the field were more actively engaged in these contexts, rather than constrained to operate within the limitations of classrooms, disciplines, and professional identifications? Our social locations will not be neat and tidy, free from contradiction, but it is imperative that we bolster efforts to facilitate learning and knowledge creation that identify the mechanisms that constrain and liberate historical memory, imagination, and consciousness.

New Directions for Adult and Continuing Education • DOI: 10.1002/ace

References

Allman, P. (2010). *Critical education against global capitalism: Karl Marx and revolutionary critical education*. Rotterdam, The Netherlands: Sense Publishers.

Baptist, W. (2010). A new and unsettling force: The strategic relevance of Rev. Dr. Martin Luther King, Jr.'s Poor People's Campaign. *Interface, 2*(1), 262–270.

Baptist, W., & Rehmann, J. (2011). *Pedagogy of the poor*. New York, NY: Teachers College Press.

Berger, D., Funke, P., & Wolfson, T. (2011). Communications networks, movements and the neoliberal city: The Media Mobilizing Project in Philadelphia. *Transforming Anthropology, 19*(2), 187–201.

Brookfield, S. D., & Holst, J. D. (2011). *Radicalizing learning: Adult education for a just world*. San Francisco, CA: Jossey-Bass.

Cohen, J., & Solomon, N. (1995). The Martin Luther King you don't see on TV. *Fairness and accuracy in reporting*. Retrieved from http://www.fair.org/index.php?page=2269

Ebert, T. L. (1996). *Ludic feminism and after: Postmodernism, desire, and labor in late capitalism*. Ann Arbor: University of Michigan Press.

Foley, G. (2001). *Learning in social action: A contribution to understanding informal education*. London, England: Zed Books.

Funke, P., Robe, C., & Wolfson, T. (2012). Suturing working class subjectivities: Media Mobilizing Project and the role of media building a class-based social movement. *Triple-C: Cognition, Communication, Co-Operation, 10*(1), 16–29.

Gilbert, M. R. (2001). From the "Walk for Adequate Welfare" to the "March for Our Lives": Welfare rights organizing in the 1960s and 1990s. *Urban Geography, 22*(5), 440–456.

Harvey, D. (2005). *A brief history of neoliberalism*. New York, NY: Oxford University Press.

Immigration and Nationality Act of 1965, Pub. L. No. 89–236, § 201, 79 Stat. 911 (1965).

Jackson, N. (1995). "These things just happen": Talk, text, and curriculum reform. In M. Campbell & A. Manicom (Eds.), *Knowledge, experience, and ruling relations* (pp. 164–180). Toronto, Ontario, Canada: University of Toronto Press.

Jesson, J., & Newman, M. (2004). Radical adult education and learning. In G. Foley (Ed.), *Dimensions of adult learning: Adult education and training in a global era* (pp. 251–264). Maidenhead, Berkshire, England: Open University Press.

Krebs, J. (1996, October 23). Homeless proclaim success, end Capitol protest. *The Patriot News*, pp. B1, B4.

Macek, S. (2006). *Urban nightmares: The media, the right, and the moral panic over the city*. Minneapolis: University of Minnesota Press.

Martin, I. (2006). In whose interests? Interrogating the metamorphosis of adult education. In A. Antikainen, P. Harinen, & C. A. Torres (Eds.), *In from the margins: Adult education, work and civil society* (pp. 11–26). Rotterdam, The Netherlands: Sense Publishers.

Mojab, S. (2009). Turning work and lifelong learning inside out: A Marxist-Feminist attempt. In L. Cooper & S. Walters (Eds.), *Learning/Work: Turning work and lifelong learning inside out* (pp. 4–15). Cape Town, South Africa: Human Sciences Research Council.

Mott, V. W. (2006). Is adult education an agent for change or instrument of the status quo? In S. B. Merriam, B. C. Courtenay, & R. M. Cervero (Eds.), *Global issues and adult education: Perspectives from Latin America, South Africa and the United States* (pp. 95–105). San Francisco, CA: Jossey-Bass.

Murray, K. (2012). Regulating activism: An institutional ethnography of public participation. *Community Development Journal, 47*(2), 199–215.

Nesbit, T. (Ed.). (2005). *New Directions for Adult and Continuing Education: No. 106. Class concerns: Adult education and social class*. San Francisco, CA: Jossey-Bass.

Preskill, S., & Brookfield, S. D. (2009). *Learning as a way of leading: Lessons from the struggle for social justice*. San Francisco, CA: Jossey-Bass.

Rankin, J. M., & Campbell, M. (2009). Institutional ethnography (IE), nursing work and hospital reform: IE's cautionary analysis. *Forum Qualitative Sozialforschung / Forum: Qualitative Social Research, 10*(2). Retrieved from http://www.qualitative-research.net/index.php/fqs/article/view/1258/2720

Sager, T. (2011). Neo-liberal urban planning policies: A literature survey 1990–2010. *ScienceDirect, 76*(4), 147–199.

Smith, N. (2002). New globalism, new urbanism: Gentrification as global urban strategy. *Antipode, 34*(3), 427–450.

Takaki, R. (1989). *Strangers from a different shore: A history of Asian Americans.* Boston, MA: Little, Brown, & Company.

Themba-Nixon, M., & Rubin, N. (2003). Speaking for ourselves: A movement led by people of color seeks media justice—not just media reform. *The Nation, 277*(16). Retrieved from http://www.thenation.com/article/speaking-ourselves

SHIVAANI A. SELVARAJ *is a doctoral candidate in the adult education program at Pennsylvania State University.*

New Directions for Adult and Continuing Education • DOI: 10.1002/ace

This chapter addresses complex dynamics and turmoil that may be unleashed when universities attempt to engage with community. Benefits and risks are examined through stories that illustrate the power and potential conflicts at the core of academic intrusions into the lives of marginalized people.

The Illusive Ground Between Town and Gown

Tom Heaney

It was a warm summer day, the sidewalks of southwest Rockford, Illinois, teaming with mothers, children, and a few men—mostly unemployed. The grandeur of this once proud neighborhood had long ago passed into neglect. Storefronts—some boarded up, one converted into a Pentecostal church, a few still open for business—underscored the pervasive poverty of neglect. Light traffic moved through the streets, weaving around potholes—one in particular that was large enough to swallow a car whole—a sinkhole that had blighted the street for over a month.

Three people stood around the sinkhole talking about their failed efforts to get the city to take action and repair this dangerous condition. Two of them were members of a local community-based organization. I was the third, a faculty member from a state university. As we plotted the next steps, I suggested a plan of action based on work undertaken by the National Film Board of Canada in the previous decade (Waugh, Brendan Baker, & Winton, 2010). The plan involved the use of a video camera as an organizing tool. Here is how it worked.

A week later, several residents stood around the sinkhole. One stood by a video camera mounted on a tripod, another held a microphone, and a third spoke with passersby about the neglect of southwest Rockford and used the sinkhole as an example. People, attracted by the apparent media presence, started drifting over to the scene to discover what was happening and in the process became engaged in conversation with each other and with the woman holding the microphone. One woman in the growing crowd even acted out for the camera by climbing into the hole until only her head and shoulders could be seen. It was hilarious, but also seriously engaged; at issue was the community

New Directions for Adult and Continuing Education, no. 139, Fall 2013 © 2013 Wiley Periodicals, Inc.
Published online in Wiley Online Library (wileyonlinelibrary.com) • DOI: 10.1002/ace.20062

demanding the same city services that were provided to their more prosperous neighbors.

Everyone who joined into this make-believe press conference was given a card as they left. The card invited them to a meeting that evening at a church down the street. People who had participated in this bit of street theater were told that the video would be shown at the meeting and there would be discussion of how to take action. Amazingly, almost 50 people attended that meeting, probably to see themselves on television! So the planning committee of three was transformed to 50 people committed to demanding that the city remove the blight of neglected streets from their neighborhood. The group relived their earlier encounter on the street through the video. They collectively identified the most significant points made on the tape, which then provided the meeting organizers with a basis for editing the tape.

The most important question, of course, was what to do with the tape. To whom should it be shown? The answer was clear. The tape should be shown to the city commissioner responsible for maintaining Rockford's streets. A meeting was set up with the commissioner and two people representing the community organization—a nonthreatening, small intrusion into the life of a busy bureaucrat. However, the threatening nature of this meeting was revealed when the visitors brought with them a small monitor and video player, and became even more evident when they produced a camera and pointed it at the commissioner. What was thought to be a simple negotiation with a few concerned community members had suddenly become a public accountability session. The camera became a weapon and the commissioner its target. The response of the commissioner, or even the nonresponse, was now to be public and would be played for all southwest Rockford to see.

The tactic worked. Within the week the city took action on repairing the street, but more important this exercise in interactive media (Niemi, 1971; Ohliger & Gueulette, 1975) provided a tool for the residents of a low-income and largely silenced neighborhood to raise the decibels of their voice so it could be heard in city hall.

The University in the Background

What did the university contribute to this? It provided an idea, borrowed from our Canadian neighbors (Evans, 1991). It provided access to funding by partnering with a community organization. It provided a camera and access to editing facilities on campus for an interactive media project. But mostly it made room for the community to organize by remaining in the background. If city officials realized that the university was actively supporting the community's action, the community would have lost its credibility, and official channels would have been opened politically to eliminate the university's influence in Rockford. It's like Myles Horton said of Highlander Folk School, a social justice leadership school that played an important role in the civil rights and labor movement in this country (personal communication, 1980), "They closed Highlander because they thought Highlander was running the Civil Rights Movement. It was only after they closed Highlander that they realized Highlander wasn't running the Movement. Black people were running it!"

Colleges and universities have their own agendas and interests that at times diverge and at times come together with the agenda of community. In the best of times, for example, Service Learning aims for a balance of interests, serving the learning needs of students while at the same time addressing the service needs of the community. However, the notion of "service" suggests doing something *for* the community, with a concomitant result of fostering the community's dependence on the service provider. In actuality, Service Learning is often directed at providing learning opportunities for those enjoying privileged access to the university while ignoring the needs of the most marginalized communities (Cunningham, 1993). McCrickard (2011) speaks of three overarching categories of participation: "non-participation whereby citizens are controlled by authority, degrees of tokenism in which influencers seek to placate the citizenry into perceiving their needs are heard, and degrees of citizen's power which result in a share of control by both parties" (p. 36).

There are situations such as the one in Rockford where the desired outcome is citizen's power, independence, and voice; where the university is not an advocate but an enabler—or as has been suggested, the university is on tap, not on top. This is what I mean by the university remaining in the background. This is not easily done as many of the university's forays into community, however well intentioned, are also motivated by the political and self-promotional purpose of cementing town/gown relations. If the aim of the institution is to establish itself as a civic leader, it would not do for the university to be perceived as taking a stand for one constituent (the citizens of southwest Rockford) and against another constituent (the city managers). As Cunningham (1993) has noted, higher education is not insulated from concepts of dominance, authority, and influence.

The question for us to ask ourselves as members of the academy, members who wear that "gown" either as armor against conflict at the core of our cities or as an invisible cloak that allows us to move surreptitiously among the demons of oppression—the question is: Whom do we choose to serve, especially when the interests of the university and the interests of the community are in conflict?

Gentrification and the Growth of a University

In the 1950s Hyde Park in Chicago was caught between two blighted areas plagued by poverty and gang violence. The University of Chicago was the largest landowner in Hyde Park and maintained an undisguised interest in protecting its investment from the largely African American neighborhoods of Kenwood and Woodlawn. As Arnold Hirsch (1998) argues, the university wielded tremendous financial and political muscle, sufficient to make Hyde Park–Kenwood one of the first "urban renewal" projects in the country. In an

New Directions for Adult and Continuing Education • DOI: 10.1002/ace

effort to avoid "white flight" and retain a professional class critical to an expanding academic institution, the university began an aggressive campaign to tear down the residences of low-income people and left acres of barren and desolate land. The plan resulted in the demolition of 20% of the buildings in Hyde Park and the relocation of 20,000 residents, mostly low-income African Americans (Hirsch, 1998).

Having succeeded in Hyde Park, the university announced its South Campus Plan—a design that would expand the university into Woodlawn, a predominantly African American neighborhood to the south across a stretch of parkland called The Midway. Gradually, over a period of 10 years and the destruction of hundreds of buildings, the university built its south campus in the open spaces created by "renewal." This put the university on a collision course with three Protestant ministers and a Catholic priest from Woodlawn who later, with the assistance of Saul Alinski, founded The Woodlawn Organization—a grassroots organization whose purpose was to combat the bulldozers and halt the gentrification of their community (Horwitt 1989; Nadeau, 1996). The Woodlawn Organization managed to slow the pace of university expansion, but the South Campus across the Midway now stands where hundreds of Woodlawn residents used to live.

This story is but one of thousands that can be told in which the interests of a university and the community clash in sometimes violent and destructive ways. Given the high stakes of managing the business of the university, one might well ask whether a higher education institution can provide a platform for anyone to work with the marginalized, impoverished, and silenced. Colleges and universities will not engage in such work when it is patently in conflict with its interests, as was the case of the University of Chicago, this despite the fact that the scholarly wisdom of the academy has much to contribute to the development of communities from the bottom up. For example, the work of University of Chicago sociologist Julius Wilson was based on studies of Woodlawn and Kenwood and has served organizers and urban planners in efforts to better understand the effects of race and class on maintaining a culture of poverty (Wilson & Taub, 2007). Since I have spent much of my earlier academic career trying to bring academic insights and wisdom into situations that the university would rather avoid, a critical lesson for me has been to keep the university in the background.

City Colleges vs. *Universidad Popular*

That lesson was learned in the early 1970s when Paulo Freire was first published in the United States (*Pedagogy of the Oppressed*). I want to take you back to that time in a story that exemplifies both the best and the worst of the ivory tower's potential for working with communities.

The story began with a grassroots center called the Latin American Coalition of Lakeview, a Chicago organization that sought to move beyond the more typical service-to-individuals model by collective organizing and direct

New Directions for Adult and Continuing Education • DOI: 10.1002/ace

action. One focus for action was the disruption of the English language program provided by the City Colleges for hundreds of Latin American immigrants. The program was deaf to community concerns, which were not limited to English as a Second Language but included gentrification, discrimination, unemployment, and political voice in an increasingly Caucasian ethnic neighborhood. Here is what was amazing to me. The coalition's organizers had read Freire before most members of the academy had—in fact, they introduced Freire to me. I was working at the City Colleges at a center that had helped the coalition set up a series of workshops on local issues. The coalition wanted a new center that would replace the City Colleges program—a center they eventually came to call *Universidad Popular*. That new center would be democratically controlled by and responsive to the community, and it would employ teachers who were committed to improving the living conditions of Latinos. They knew that when people learned to read words that were charged with political significance, and when those words reflected their own experiences in community, then learning would inspire action and democratic change. They learned that from Freire.

So several of us from the City Colleges began working with the coalition to create an alternative to a citywide program run by our own higher educational institution. Amazing, since creating an independent, grassroots program would run counter to the interests of the City Colleges! Nonetheless, we succeeded in getting grants and state funding—the grants went to the coalition, but unfortunately the state funding went to the City Colleges. On the positive side, *Universidad Popular* was up and running with a community board, teachers who were from and committed to the community, and a growing realization in that community that this program was committed not only to students, but to changing conditions in their neighborhood.

That was the positive side. But on the negative side, the involvement of the City Colleges in the development of this new program brought with it the crippling demands of a multicampus, citywide bureaucracy, which was the recipient of federal and state dollars on behalf of the program. We were *not* in the background. We, who represented the City Colleges in the program, were not just providers of support and behind-the-scenes counsel; we were a fiscal agent. Even the most fundamental assumptions of those of us who planned the program had to be renegotiated with City College policy makers and also the chancellor. For example, the coalition wanted full-time and committed teachers. However, City College policy required that *their* "training specialists" not teach more than 12 hours a week—a policy that made these teachers ineligible for union membership.

Universidad Popular was about to lose its independence. The *Universidad's* board demanded that the chancellor honor earlier commitments and be accountable to the community. They organized a community-wide meeting with the chancellor to make their voices heard. Over 200 students and community residents attended. The chancellor and his entourage were amazed to see such an outpouring of interest in a 4-month-old adult education program.

New Directions for Adult and Continuing Education • DOI: 10.1002/ace

The *Universidad's* board controlled the agenda, allowing students and local leaders ample time to voice their concerns before the chancellor was given the podium.

A Design for Failure

As formidable as the chancellor was, he seldom allowed himself to be seen as the community's adversary. He preferred the role of patronizing benefactor, strengthening a dependency that tied "his" program to him. He feigned impatience with the shortsightedness of the college presidents and vice-chancellors who he brought in tow whose missteps required his intervention. He acceded to the demands of the community, promising that the community "advisory" board would guide him. He used a ploy that I had seen him use on other occasions. He observed the direction in which the people were moving, and then ran to the front to be seen as leading them in the same direction.

You can see how none of this inspired affection on the part of City College bureaucrats, either for the program or for those of us in the City Colleges who had given birth to this headache! Unfortunately, this meeting became a recurring pattern for the next 9 years. Annual crises induced by bureaucratic, administrative decisions required additional meetings with growing numbers of community residents, politicians, and public officials in attendance. Crisis management was in the hands of the chancellor who resolved the immediate issues but in the end left policies and procedures unchanged, which led inevitably to further conflict after the current conflict seemed to have been resolved. Besides, the chancellor's management by intervention heightened the hostility of lower-ranking administrators whose decisions were more likely to affect day-to-day operations at *Universidad Popular*.

Despite the ongoing tensions, the work of *Universidad Popular* prospered. In addition to the English as a Second Language and other basic education classes, the program offered workshops on family planning, the prevention of child and spouse abuse, the elimination of drug abuse, and health care. A theater group presented plays about life in the community and another program offered free legal counseling. Spanish classes were also offered for Anglo-Americans, many of them professionals who would help the program through the difficult years ahead. There were frequent fiestas that made Latino culture a source of pride and joy for many racial and ethnic residents of Lakeview.

Free of a Strangling Embrace

But 10 years of struggling with the City Colleges had taught *Universidad Popular* the dangers of co-optation and dependency that can result from partnering with an academic institution. And with this realization came the inevitable conclusion; to be free the program had to leave the strangling embrace of the City Colleges. After 10 years, the program shut the door on close to $250,000 in annual funding and became what it had sought to be from its beginning: an

New Directions for Adult and Continuing Education • DOI: 10.1002/ace

independent, community-based organization. That was 1981. I recall that story today, because in May of 2012 I participated in the 40th-anniversary celebration of *Universidad Popular,* sharing memories with many of the staff from 4 decades ago about this amazing, long-lived program and the college system that almost destroyed it. I have continued to both support and learn from *Universidad Popular,* while the two universities with which I have been affiliated after leaving the City Colleges have remained in the background.

The Limits of University/Community Partnerships

Universities and community colleges claim to value community service and employ a number of strategies to reach out beyond the academy. The question we need to ask, however, is which communities is it in the interest of the university to serve? In addition, the interests of community are as complex as the interests of the university. A college or university can provide language or literacy classes for Latinos, but the interests of the Latino communities that are engaged in struggles with immigration, unemployment, police harassment, and gang violence include language and literacy—and also include so much more. Involvement in such communities frequently requires taking sides in conflicts where powerful interests are at stake.

Can a university stay in the background and take sides at the same time? The story of the interactive media project with which I began suggests that it can. However, when community service takes the form of public relations, then the university is foregrounded; it must be circumspect in its encounters with the community, measured in its response to latent conflict, and balanced in its allegiance to factions with a divided community. The university maintains an abiding interest in controlling the content it provides through its programs and initiatives. It is drawn to a service model for that very reason. But communities that seek control over the decisions that affect their day-to-day welfare and over their own learning are not likely candidates for community services of the university.

A university can take a different approach to community partnership, and at times has done so. It can assist, without controlling, communities that seek to organize locally controlled education, cultural events, or resident-managed housing. There were faculty members at the University of Chicago in the 1960s who supported The Woodlawn Organization in its efforts to halt their university's planned gentrification (Hirsch, 1998). Although a university can do these things, such efforts are unlikely to be official initiatives or administratively sanctioned. Such an approach is more likely to be taken by socially committed faculty and students who operate on their own and in the background.

Contrasting Approaches

Several years ago I was working with a group of residents of Dearborn Homes, a public housing development on the south side of Chicago. The residents were organizing to take over the management of their development, and the Chicago Housing Authority required that they first complete a feasibility study. They asked for my help. Together we decided to turn the task into a participatory research project, with the residents learning from residents like themselves who had successfully developed resident management in other cities—Boston, Newark, and St. Louis. They documented what these residents had done, planned the steps they would take at Dearborn, developed a timeline, and identified the resources and skills that would be required. Individuals volunteered to be trained in accounting, management, security, and maintenance. When they were finished a year later, they had established the feasibility of their project and had a blueprint for its implementation.

I contrast this with the more typical consulting practice of a faculty member at a neighboring university. He too was asked to assist with the development of a feasibility study for another public housing development, Wentworth Gardens, a mile distant from Dearborn Homes. However, unlike the participatory process that fully engaged the residents and left them with a document owned by the community, his approach was more academic. He and his staff wrote the feasibility study for the residents. The study was sufficient to gain the nod from the Housing Authority, but the residents had not learned from the process or acquired the skills they would need to move ahead. They could read the document of course, but the words were not theirs. Two years later, Wentworth Gardens was "resident managed," although in actuality the residents had hired a managing agency to run their development, whereas the residents of Dearborn Homes employed fellow residents in key positions. At Dearborn, the feasibility study was kept up-to-date and remained their blueprint for action.

These two contrasting approaches demonstrate a potential role for nurturing agency and change in communities of poverty and neglect. In the first example, the interaction of university and community is participatory and the university remains in the background. In the second, a more traditional consulting relationship between university and community foregrounds the university as the purveyor of expert knowledge. Only in the first is the community itself the agent of social and political change. Honoring the independent agency of democratically controlled communities is the only sustaining gift the university can bring to its neighbors. And it is in many instances the only way that the institutional interests of the university can be maintained.

References

Cunningham, P. (1993). Let's get real: A critical look at the practice of adult education. *Journal of Adult Education, 22*(1), 3–15.

Evans, G. (1991). *In the national interest: A chronicle of the National Film Board of Canada from 1949 to 1989.* Toronto, Ontario, Canada: University of Toronto Press.

Freire, P. (1970). *Pedagogy of the oppressed.* New York, NY: Seabury Press.

Hirsch, A. (1998). *Making the second ghetto: Race and housing in Chicago 1940–1960.* Chicago, IL: University of Chicago Press.
Horwitt, S. D. (1989). *Let them call me rebel: Saul Alinsky: His life and legacy.* New York, NY: Alfred A. Knopf.
McCrickard, M. (2011). *Listening to the community: An appreciative case study of service learning initiatives within a higher education institution* (Doctoral dissertation, National Louis University). Retrieved from http://digitalcommons.nl.edu/diss/47/
Nadeau, D. (1996). *Counting our victories: Popular education and organizing.* Westminster, British Columbia, Canada: Media Resources for Mobilization.
Niemi, J. (1971). *Mass media and adult education.* Englewood Cliffs, NJ: Educational Technology Publications.
Ohliger, J., & Gueulette, D. (1975). *Media and adult learning: A bibliography with abstracts, annotations, and quotations.* New York, NY: Garland Publishing.
Waugh, T., Brendan Baker, M., & Winton, E. (Eds.). (2010). *Challenge for change: Activist documentary at the National Film Board of Canada.* Kingston, Ontario, Canada: McGill-Queen's University Press.
Wilson, W. J., & Taub, R. P. (2007). *There goes the neighborhood: Racial, ethnic, and class tensions in four Chicago neighborhoods and their meaning for America.* New York, NY: Vintage.

TOM HEANEY *is an associate professor at National Louis University and director of the adult and continuing education doctoral program.*

5

In this chapter, four longtime adult literacy practitioners recount their pathways into the field in the late 1970s, 1980s, and early 1990s. Their stories highlight the creativity and openness that characterized literacy work in those years and point to what has been lost as the field has become dominated by the Workforce Investment Act and the National Reporting System.

The Turtle's Shell: Protecting the Life Underneath

John Garvey, John Gordon, Peter Kleinbard, Paul Wasserman

One thing I think we've been able to do is to create and preserve what I call protected spaces. There has been, and continues to be, a core of folks throughout New York's literacy world who are fiercely committed to the founding ideals of the field. In the face of an increasingly regressive policy environment; woefully inadequate and incoherent funding streams; and distorted, dishonest data regimes, many adult education administrators have served as a kind of buffer between these larger forces and the day-to-day work of teachers and students. It's a tricky balancing act, and it's easy to lose clarity or to give in to what often feels like insurmountable pressures to join the chorus insisting that the emperor really is wearing clothes. But to date, within the City's literacy system, there still is some precious space to do high-quality instructional work in classrooms and whole programs, work that honors, respects and supports our students—folks from the city's poor, immigrant and working class communities who come to us to further their educations, often with the deeper hope that we can help them transform their lives.

Paul Wasserman

On August 7, 1998, President Bill Clinton signed the Workforce Investment Act into law. The law, in its own words, create(d) an integrated, "one-stop" system of workforce investment and education activities for adults and youth. The Workplace Investment Act consolidated policies that had been developing for some time and ushered in the National Reporting System—ultimately transforming the landscape of adult literacy education.

NEW DIRECTIONS FOR ADULT AND CONTINUING EDUCATION, no. 139, Fall 2013 © 2013 Wiley Periodicals, Inc.
Published online in Wiley Online Library (wileyonlinelibrary.com) • DOI: 10.1002/ace.20063

In the years since, adult education has increasingly been defined almost solely as a means to produce workers for the U.S. economy, and that vision, shaped by a very narrow set of skills and outcomes, has come to seem almost incontrovertible.

But adult literacy work has not always been that way. This article, through the stories of four individuals active in the field for many years, reaches back to a key period in literacy work in New York City: the late 1970s through the early 1990s. Literacy programs dramatically expanded in those years, bringing into the field many practitioners with little or no background in adult education, but with a wide range of experiences in the community. Those individuals had come of age in the 1960s and early 1970s, and their worldviews had been shaped by the events of that era, most especially by the civil rights movement. They saw their literacy work within a broader social vision and brought egalitarian instincts and perspectives to their classrooms. They believed that education had a broad mission to encourage active, thoughtful civic participation. There was a ferment and spirit of exploration, enabled in part by the new funds and an openness at all levels of those involved. Teachers and administrators studied, experimented, shared ideas and practices, and engaged students in shaping teaching and learning—in the process contributing to, as well as consuming, the base of knowledge in the field.

Three of the four participants, John Garvey, John Gordon, and Paul Wasserman, worked as cab drivers in New York City during the 1970s. All were active in the Taxi Rank and File Coalition, an insurgent group within the industry formed in response to the terrible wages and working conditions and the incredible lack of democracy within the taxi workers' union.

John Gordon

Many of us had been active in the antiwar and other movements of the 1960s, and our approach to taxi organizing was significantly shaped by that experience. In particular, we were committed to practicing a kind of participatory democracy and nonhierarchical organization. We were acutely aware of the ways that the voices of rank-and-file drivers had been silenced and ignored by both the taxi owners and the union bosses. We saw our role, in part, as creating a space for those voices to be heard.

We believed in another 1960s axiom: that the personal is political, that the way we interacted with each other—the kind of community we built— was a critical part of our political practice. All these ideas would later find resonance in my literacy work.

John Garvey

By 1978, I was ready to stop driving. A short time earlier, I had begun working part-time as a tutor in a writing center of a City University of New York

(CUNY) college. I responded to a newspaper ad for a tutor in an adult basic education program at a city jail, sponsored by what was then New York City Community College—in part because I was attracted to the political potentials of getting to know people behind bars. Fortunately, my employment application fell upon the desk of an extraordinary educator, Fannie Eisenstein, who persuaded the college's employment office that I had exactly the right credentials for the job. Soon afterward, I entered the Brooklyn House of Detention on Atlantic Avenue.

John Gordon

I came into literacy work in 1985 with the wave of new programs started when the mayor allocated $35 million over 4 years to the expansion of adult literacy programs in New York City. I had no formal teaching experience before coming into literacy. I had been working for the previous 6 years as a machinist and the 7 years before that as a Yellow Cab driver.

In 1984, I was looking for a change and thinking about teaching. When a position opened up as Teacher–Coordinator of the Open Book, the newly funded literacy program of Good Shepherd Services, I applied. Somehow they hired me.

I was drawn to literacy work partially because I had a sense of its transformative possibilities. I thought that in bringing people together to study and learn, we would find opportunities to read and write about things that mattered to students and in the process develop new senses of ourselves and our possibilities.

Peter Kleinbard

In 1984, I was asked to start a school for youth 16 to 24 years old who had dropped out—what became known as the Young Adult Learning Academy (YALA). My experience teaching in the performing arts had focused on bringing together diverse groups of youth at an integrated but racially divided school, Berkeley High School in California. At the time, I believed that racial inequities were on their way to major improvement, and that my part was to be in the schools. My specific interests were in the arts, building social capital (Coleman, 1981), and creating communities (Shils, 1975).

Paul Wasserman

When I entered the adult literacy world in September 1991, it was still pulsating with the 1960s-flavored ideals that infused its early years but increasingly buffeted by bureaucratic and political headwinds from the institutional settings in which it was embedded.

I had decided to become a teacher 4 years earlier. After a couple of months trudging through the bureaucratic marshland of the (then) Board of Education, and a semester of substitute teaching, I landed a job as a social studies teacher at Bronx Outreach, a "second chance" alternative high school for 17- to 21-year-olds. My time there provided a rich learning experience about teaching and classroom management; about the lives and minds of Bronx young people; about the mix of cultures, races, and ethnicities that populated the borough; and about the choking limitations on good educational practice imposed by bureaucratic structures and mind-sets.

After 3 years, I was feeling increasingly frustrated by those limitations, with little room for implementing the kind of alternative educational practices I had been exposed to, particularly the idea of theme-based instruction.

At the time, my Taxi Rank and File comrade, John Garvey, was overseeing an overhaul of CUNY's campus-based General Educational Development programs, reshaping them around a theme-based interdisciplinary model. He told me that the Institute for Literacy Studies at Lehman College, where I had taken an inspiring semester-long workshop, was looking for a part-time teacher/director to help develop and run their new General Educational Development program. This was too perfect a fit to ignore.

John Garvey

The Brooklyn House is an 11-story building that probably housed about 700 to 800 adult men—virtually all of whom were in jail because they were not able to make bail on various felony charges. Complaints about the lawyers were numerous and many inmates spent hours in the jail's law library in an effort to help themselves. In the end, the great majority of them "copped a plea" rather than go to trial in what they saw as a realistic assessment of their chances of being set free in as little time as possible.

Teaching in a jail is not quite like teaching elsewhere, not even in a prison. First off, the inmates were endlessly coming and going—sometimes as the result of changes in their status, other times due to the quite arbitrary decision-making of the Department of Correction authorities. Stable enrollments were elusive. In addition, most of the guards were not especially sympathetic to classes for individuals who they perceived as lowlifes and losers. In light of the pervasive negative attitudes, perhaps what was most surprising was the presence of a few officers who were genuinely supportive.

I was not ready to do as well as I needed to. A couple of my first students really didn't know how to read at all. In my desperate, and quite ignorant, efforts to figure out what to do, I prepared flash cards for them to look at and call out the words—simply because I remembered using flash cards myself as a child. I wish I could do most of it over again.

I did get to join a remarkable group of people at the college who were intensely devoted to their work and their students—people who have made remarkable differences in the lives of individual students and contributed to the enrichment of a broad range of educational institutions and programs across several decades.

New Directions for Adult and Continuing Education • DOI: 10.1002/ace

In some instances, the practices in the college were fairly advanced but, in other cases, they were grounded in what now appears to me to be a somewhat limited understanding of the complexities of effective literacy instruction. In general, the teachers were granted considerable independence in the classroom. In retrospect, I imagine that our primary consideration in the evaluation of teaching was the extent to which teachers seemed able to organize their lessons in a coherent manner, provide good explanations, and engage their students.

John Gordon

I didn't know much about adult education practice at the time, but even to my unsophisticated eyes the instructional materials I could find seemed impoverished. I remember ordering materials from some of the adult education publishing houses and being struck by how poor they were—dry, boring workbooks on topics like how to get and keep a job (Don't yell at the boss!). And the reading materials were for the most part so bland that I couldn't imagine students getting excited by them. I could find no sense of the potential for literacy to open up new worlds or help students reimagine their own.

On the other hand, the field in New York City seemed wide open. The sudden expansion of adult literacy services in the city had brought in a lot of new teachers who weren't committed to conventional methods. Staff and students at programs around the city were experimenting with different approaches to teaching, finding ways to situate curriculum in students' lived experience, and rethinking the student–teacher relationship.

Staff at Literacy Volunteers, for example, was developing student-centered approaches to writing instruction. Students at Bronx Educational Services were working as assistant teachers. The Institute for Literacy Studies at Lehman College sponsored conferences that brought students and teachers together to explore collaborative approaches to teaching and learning. Adult education students formed an independent citywide student organization: Adult United Voices.

This was just a piece of what was going on in New York City. After all, there were some 50,000 students in literacy, General Educational Development (GED), and English to Speakers of Other Languages classes citywide. Still, I believe that period was characterized by a sense of excitement and engagement with questions of teaching and learning and how those things might be meaningfully connected to people's daily lives—a sharp contrast to the current situation where the National Reporting System and the focus on testing have pushed essential questions of teaching and learning, relevance, and meaning to the back burner.

Peter Kleinbard

YALA was envisioned by Marian Schwartz, in Mayor Koch's office, as a model for youth with very poor academic skills who had dropped out. Just as they

New Directions for Adult and Continuing Education • DOI: 10.1002/ace

do today, these youths represented by far the majority of dropouts. Their prospects were dim in the economy of the time, but less dim than those facing similar youth today.

In the 1980s, the major policy vehicles for young dropouts were shaped by the view that long-term and comprehensive services were a waste. "They had their chance and they blew it," was the line. Low-literacy youth were rarely served in employment programs because of the time and costs required to attain a GED or job, much the same as today.

Those designing YALA understood that for young adults to advance, they must be supported comprehensively, addressing personal, social, and academic development. The school was structured as a partnership between an educational program and eight community-based organizations. These organizations were to recruit youth in their communities and provide counseling, work preparation (including internships with stipends), and job placement.

YALA had extensive resources, but its funding agencies, structure, and scale required figuring out a lot of new challenges. Many of its shaping ideas became important in later years when New York City developed large numbers of small high schools and Multiple Pathways schools and programs (2003 forward): partnerships with CBOs and integration of work experience within an educational setting.

Initially, we focused on increasing student participation and engagement, and creating an orderly and constructive culture in which all felt secure. We sought to understand and address student needs and strengths with the rough tools we had and refined the program each cycle. At the time, few in the literacy community had much appetite for young dropouts. Leaders from the Literacy Assistance Center, CUNY, and the Mayor's Office helped improve the alignment between the different funding agencies and the goals of YALA. The Board of Education sent instructors who were not suited to YALA students, and their union affiliation made it difficult to get the level of work we needed from them. With the support of the Mayor's Office, I was empowered to hire appropriate teachers and get them licensed. Many talented and caring individuals began to form a staff. Significant numbers were people of color, something that the students and the community-based organizations cited as a strength.

The Department of Employment (DOE) required that youth be placed in jobs within several months of entering YALA. Trying to keep youth longer was in this view, to quote one of the DOE staff, "an invitation for them to get in trouble" (she meant in the old sense of girls becoming pregnant). Again, the Mayor's Office forced DOE to allow youth to remain longer.

As these changes took place, there remained much work to do on the ground. A key indicator, student attendance, showed consistent improvement. Cooperation among school and CBO staff improved, though there were outliers. There were lots of events, opportunities to eat together, recognition ceremonies, and student publications including the annual *YALA Journal*. YALA began to function as a school and a community.

New Directions for Adult and Continuing Education • DOI: 10.1002/ace

Paul Wasserman

I began my work at Lehman seeing myself primarily as a teacher, and have tried to keep that sense of my identity front and center even as the balance between my teaching and administrative roles tilted increasingly toward the administrative. Even before I started at Lehman, the program's philosophy was that administrators should also teach, and we've sustained that as a core structure and value. To me, the evolution of the adult literacy workforce into a core of reasonably well-paid program and system administrators, mostly detached from the classroom, on the one hand, and a mostly part-time and poorly paid army of teachers on the other, has been a key marker of the field's move away from the alternative and toward the institutional.

Since my days of taxi driving, I've carried a basic skepticism about all institutionalized structures, including those in the education and nonprofit worlds. So, while acknowledging the good and necessary work these institutions may be doing, I think it's also important to see them in a parallel framework as agencies of social control. Folks like us, who've found comfortable careers within these institutions, are caught in a constant tension—between being facilitators of righteous, liberatory work on the one hand, and being implementers (however reluctantly) of social control over poor and working-class people on the other hand.

John Garvey

During my first few years of working in the jails, it was common to come across newspaper articles suggesting that much criminal activity was due to the poor literacy skills of the individuals involved or, in another version, to undetected learning disabilities. For a number of reasons, most important my everyday encounters with individuals behind bars, this explanation increasingly made little sense. It seemed to me that criminal activity was a much more complex affair. I was especially skeptical of accounts that left out any consideration of the workings of multiple racist institutions when, even then, the jails and prisons were filled with Black and Hispanic men. I began poking around for different ways of thinking about the issues. Literacy and language seemed to be key.

If we can become accustomed to using language and literacy in many different ways, we can imagine ourselves acting in many different ways in the world. Truth be told, it may happen the other way around—if we have the opportunity to act in many different ways, we may acquire many different uses of language and literacy. In any case, there's a relationship between what we do and our "ways with words" (Heath, 1983).

In jails and prisons, there's a real limit to how much individuals can change what they do (although there are any number of remarkable accounts of individuals who refused to let the routines of custody determine who they were: Malcolm X; the boxer Hurricane Carter; or even in a very different context, the Birdman of Alcatraz, Robert Stroud. But you can change what you do with words. Becoming more versatile with the ways that words can be used can lay the basis for becoming more capable at negotiating difficult circumstances outside. Ultimately, new ways with words can lead to imagining new ways of acting—possibly even including political ways. But, and this is a really big "but," an unchanged world will all but always limit the potential and significance of those new ways of acting.

Years later, when I was at CUNY's Office of Academic Affairs, we published a small book titled *In Their Own Eyes: Self Portraits of Adult Students* (Division of Adult and Continuing Education, 1995), which captured the ways in which students made sense of their own often painful experiences in life and schools. Students who contributed their accounts frequently spoke about the ways in which their participation in literacy classes had affected their abilities to speak in the world—most significantly, they talked about the ways in which their participation in genuine communicative activities in classes allowed them to become more able to participate in real discussions outside of class.

Paul Wasserman

As a teacher, my initial focus was on teaching content; on exposing students to new ideas and perspectives about the world; and on providing opportunities for them to develop their own voices and ideas while engaging them in enjoyable and meaningful reading, writing, and classroom activities—with content learning as the primary goal.

But I soon realized that the issue of skill development also needed attention. Much of my growth as a teacher has involved viewing work with students through both a content and a literacy lens, and I've been fortunate to work closely with some of the city's most skilled and knowledgeable literacy practitioners. CUNY's move toward theme-based curricula and instruction in part involved shifting instructional work away from teaching discrete, decontextualized skills toward a focus on rich content learning, with skill development embedded in and growing out of content-based instruction. In some ways, I needed to make the opposite shift—to pay careful attention to coherent skill and literacy development and to see that as equally important as content learning.

I've also learned an incredible amount from students, who bring a wealth of life experience, wisdom, and passion into the classroom, but who also have huge gaps in basic skills, writing facility, and background knowledge. Understanding these gaps and trying to develop strategies to address them has been a central part of our work at Lehman and in CUNY.

While literacy work in New York City was well established when I started, the process of redesigning GED work in CUNY felt fresh and exciting, with a sense that we were doing important, innovative work. For me, it serves as a powerful model of collaborative, system-wide program development.

New Directions for Adult and Continuing Education • DOI: 10.1002/ace

Despite institutional and budgetary limitations, there was lots of room for creative play. John had created a foundation of structures and guiding principles but left space for experimentation at the program level and for feedback from and dialogue between teachers and administrators. At Lehman, too, we were given freedom to develop our program creatively, which we did over the course of several years, through a rich, collaborative process.

Peter Kleinbard

As director of YALA, I saw my role as creating a setting that would encourage good things to happen. I focused on hiring and supporting instructors who could address skills and encourage active roles for young people while demonstrating that adults could have positive and creative lives.

We built a small unit structure with teams comprising CBO counselors and teachers working with small groups of youth. We encouraged a focus on individual students at regular meetings of these teams. I sought out for leadership roles staff that could complement my strengths and compensate for my lacks. The deputy director took the lead on student disciplinary issues. Several experienced instructors worked to strengthen instruction school-wide by drawing upon research and practice in literacy.

In 1994, however, after Rudy Giuliani became Mayor, essential supports were stripped away. Most important was the ability to hire suitable teachers. The YALA staff had been painstakingly assembled, had built a professional community, and had developed the skills to work well with the CBOs. These were displaced by Board of Education instructors selected because of seniority, many of them individuals who had not fared well in teaching positions previously. We fought these changes. A teacher led a sit-in at City Hall, and I reached out to leaders in the administration and union. But this was to no avail. Deeply disappointed in the undermining of YALA, and the many disturbing events that occurred as a result, I felt helpless to turn things around and moved on in 1996.

John Gordon

The Open Book was located in Brooklyn—in a neighborhood that would go through a period of intense gentrification over the next 15 years. Many of the students were single mothers on public assistance, living in the surrounding neighborhoods and fighting to stay in their homes. They didn't have much confidence in themselves as students, but they arrived at the Open Book with a lot of life experience and they weren't shy. Our classroom was quickly bubbling over with the day-to-day stories of their lives. It didn't take long for those stories to make their way into our reading and writing and for the students to make the space their own. The story of the Open Book is told in much fuller detail elsewhere (Evans, Gordon, & Ramdeholl, 2009; Gordon & Ramdeholl, 2010).

New Directions for Adult and Continuing Education • DOI: 10.1002/ace

Before long, we started holding monthly meetings at the school. Students played an important role in shaping curriculum, determining the class structure and schedule, and hiring teachers. We began recording and publishing oral histories in which students explored critical issues such as domestic violence, alcohol and substance abuse, and their struggles in school. As we groped our way toward a coherent pedagogy, writing and student publishing became a central part of our curriculum.

Over time we assembled a strong staff, but we were acutely aware that we had a lot to learn and read everything we could get our hands on. We gravitated toward building curriculum around student-identified themes, partly because it fit with our notion of the Open Book as a learning community, but also because it seemed to make more sense to teach skills in context and to expose students to authentic texts and real literature, texts that would get them excited about reading and help them find real purpose in getting better at it.

I came to see the Open Book as a place that, in some small way, functioned as an alternative to the dominant culture, a place that students could shape according to values that were important to them; a culture they could participate in actively as opposed to the enforced passivity of the mainstream; and a place where they could engage in the practice of democracy, and in that process come to see themselves in new and different ways.

Conclusion

We began this chapter with the observation that implementation of the National Reporting System and the increasing focus on preparation for work has led to a narrowing of the space available for adult educators to develop approaches that engage students as active participants in their own learning, a key to developing powerful literacy and language skills. That narrowing is, of course, a reality at all levels of education. In K–12, as well as adult education, the mantra of "college and career readiness" serves as the organizing principle of much educational "reform." Test-based accountability models increasingly dominate K–12 education, triggering widespread concern by teachers, students, and parents about the narrowing of the curriculum, while distracting from other evidence of growth. As Koretz (2010) of Harvard University points out, the negative impact of test-based accountability goes even deeper, because it often generates "substantial distortions of practice . . . and inflation of test scores, that is, increases in scores larger than the actual improvements in the latent proficiencies the tests are intended to estimate" (p. 4).

In New York, we see this process manifest itself in the annual report cards issued to adult education programs by the New York State Education Department, with the distortions accentuated by the pressure that programs are under to massage data in order to receive high report-card grades. These are disconnected from descriptions of actual practice, thus revealing little about program quality—but perhaps more about adeptness at getting the numbers right. While more program resources and management time are devoted to

New Directions for Adult and Continuing Education • DOI: 10.1002/ace

playing with data, less go to instruction and teacher support. Fewer programs offer classes for lower-level students, for whom large educational gains and outcomes such as the GED take longer to achieve. These, the very folks for whom the field of adult education was developed, are a shrinking presence in our world.

We believe that adult education would be well served if teachers and students became engaged actively in efforts to explore and understand these trends, and to reclaim the right to define the purposes of our work and to shape the learning communities in which we come together. We hope that our reflections prove helpful to that effort.

References

Coleman, J. S. (1981). *The adolescent society: The social life of the teenager and its impact on education*. Westport, CT: Greenwood Publishers.

Division of Adult and Continuing Education. (1995). *In their own eyes: Self-portraits of adult students*. New York, NY: NYS Literacy Resource Center.

Evans, S., Gordon, J., & Ramdeholl, D. (2009). Making a beach: Women, community, and democracy at the Open Book. In M. Miller & K. P. King (Eds.), *Empowering women through literacy: Views from experience* (pp. 221–232). Charlotte, NC: Information Age Publishing.

Gordon, J., & Ramdeholl, D. (2010). Everybody had a piece: Collaborative practice and shared decision making at the Open Book. In D. Ramdeholl, T. Giordani, T. Heaney, & W. Yanow (Eds.), *New Directions for Adult and Continuing Education: No. 128. The struggle for democracy in adult education* (pp. 27–35). San Francisco, CA: Jossey-Bass.

Heath, S. B. (1983). *Ways with words: Language, life, and work in communities and classrooms.* Cambridge, England: Cambridge University Press.

Koretz, D. (2010). *Implications of current policy for education measurement.* Princeton, NJ: Education Testing Service.

Shils, E. (1975). *Center and periphery: Essays on macrosociology: Selected papers of Edward Shils.* Chicago, IL: University of Chicago Press.

JOHN GARVEY has been involved in literacy-connected education work for more than 30 years in New York.

JOHN GORDON left the Open Book in 2000. He now works at the Fortune Society.

PETER KLEINBARD is conducting research on youth who have dropped out and the organizations that serve them, following many years of direct service and program development support for programs that serve adolescents and young adults.

PAUL WASSERMAN retired as director of the Lehman College Adult Learning Center in the Bronx in 2011, but continues to teach at the program part-time.

6

This chapter describes how the author became an academic political educator and community organizer, with both worlds always working with, against, and for each other.

Two Worlds in One Backpack

Mechthild Hart

"Why Are You an Academic?"

When I was invited to speak on a panel called "Reaching Out Beyond the Ivory Tower" at the 2012 Adult Education Research Conference and sat down to think about what I would say, what immediately came to mind was the question I was asked by a community organizer. Driving her home from a meeting and talking about our political work, all of a sudden she asked me: "Why are you an academic?"

I don't remember exactly what I said in response to this question. I do, however, remember trying to explain why the two worlds implied in her question— the world of political organizing and the world of academe—have never really been that separate for me. No matter in which of the two worlds I may be moving at a particular time, the other world is always with me. Both are part of the "essential belongings" (Braidotti, 1994) that I carry with me, all tucked away in one backpack.

Throughout my life journey across geographical distances, cultures, languages, and classes, as well as political and academic boundaries, I have been filling this backpack with what were to become my various essential belongings. In this essay I trace my journey from where and how it started, and how the journey has become a way of "playful 'world'-traveling" (Lugones, 2003, p. 78).

Beginnings

I grew up after WWII in a family that was quite poor. My mother sustained us with what I later learned to identify as a "subsistence orientation toward life." I remember her never-ending care work, and my own endless participation in

NEW DIRECTIONS FOR ADULT AND CONTINUING EDUCATION, no. 139, Fall 2013 © 2013 Wiley Periodicals, Inc.
Published online in Wiley Online Library (wileyonlinelibrary.com) • DOI: 10.1002/ace.20064

all her efforts. I also remember my regular attempts to escape, to hide in dark corners where my parents could not find me right away and chase me back to the kitchen or garden. In my hiding places I read anything our church library had to offer. Later, as a high school student, I read a lot of literature considered part of European High Culture. By then a profound passion for reading had become one of my essential belongings.

Then I discovered another book in my parents' small library at home. Mixed in with the novels that my mother liked to read I found a book on Nazi medical experiments on Jews in concentration camps. Reading about these unspeakable horrors, and realizing that ordinary Germans condoned, ignored, or silenced them, shaped another one of my essential belongings: an acute knowledge and painful awareness of the horrors of anti-Semitism. Many years later this knowledge was enlarged, branched out into learning about other kinds and histories of racism, and how my own heritage as a German and as a White person has always been deeply implicated in these horrors.

My father insisted that I get a university education, one that he had always wanted for himself but could not afford, his parents just making do with their small bakery in a small village in southern Germany. I moved to Munich and studied literature and music. I always did the work for my music classes, but I hardly ever showed up for the lectures on German literature, too tired to get up after late-night movies or sitting around with friends after our weekly visit to the opera or a concert. One morning, when I did show up, I saw a bunch of students storming into the lecture hall and surrounding the professor, stopping him from continuing his "reactionary fascist propaganda," urging us to boycott his lectures.

When I asked one of my fellow students what this was all about, she gave me a book on Marx and Engels and asked me to come to a women's reading group she attended every week. All the women had boyfriends who had read Marx and the neo-Marxists, and who were directly involved in organizing various political demonstrations and interruptions of university life. Their girlfriends had to catch up on their knowledge of Marxist theories. I was the only one who did not have a boyfriend, but I was probably in love with the friend who asked me to join.

We read Marx's *Early Manuscripts*, and at times we spent hours discussing just one or two paragraphs, probing into the depth of its meaning, looking at it from all sorts of angles.

So, there were the pleasures of carefully, diligently thinking and analyzing, always accompanied by laughter, pastry, and coffee. This is how reading and constructing theory evolved into another one of my passions and became another one of my essential belongings.

Becoming an Academic Political Educator

Marrying an American academic meant moving to a small Midwestern town, with a middle-class academic ghetto on one side (which I was told is called a

New Directions for Adult and Continuing Education • DOI: 10.1002/ace

"campus") and a real town inhabited by "nonacademics" on the other. This was in 1972, just at the peak of the women's movement. I continued to study German literature, but I also became involved in feminist movement politics, first in the founding of a women's bookstore and then of a shelter for battered women.

This was also the time I decided to have a child. And when she arrived, one grand new world opened up and a few others collapsed. I was moved into the inner workings of care work, and it was made painfully clear to me that this was "women's work" that neither academia nor my academic husband had any interest in.

My on-the-ground political work had already touched the nerve that keeps animating my longing and passion for education, and my conviction that education is one of the most peaceful, constructive ways of changing minds and worlds. Somehow I no longer saw any meaning in becoming a professor of German literature. When someone told me about the existence of an adult education program, I thought that going there would allow me to merge my political work with my intellectual work, my being a political activist with being a political scholar, all bunched up in being a political educator.

To my surprise, my belief in being able to apply previous political–academic training of always critically probing into what people (my adult education professors included) were talking about burst like a soap bubble. As I saw it, adult education literature at that time was just old White boys preaching about their particular notion of common sense, clearly not seeing, or leaving entirely untouched the world of economic exploitation, class divisions, and cultural imperialism. Borrowing from one of June Jordan's early poems, "I became a menace to my enemies" (Jordan, 2005, p. 170), and I spare the reader the details of that part of the story where I was shut down, literally asked to drop a class because my political views had no place in "a middle-class institution," and of various other attempts to make me leave the program.

I did not say much, but I learned to write papers that continued to radically question taken-for-granted assumptions with carefully laid-out arguments, all plentifully referenced. This was my way of self-defense, of shouting "Don't touch me, I am as academic as can be, despite of, or in conjunction with my political radicalism!" It also gave me great joy since it allowed me to indulge in my passion for theory.

I wrote my dissertation *Towards a Theory of Collective Learning* (Hart, 1987), instigated by my experiences in the battered women's collective. The collective made decisions by consensus, and I often saw people agree to something in tears, and after long hours of debates which I later learned to understand as communicative power moves. I turned to the German political theorist Jürgen Habermas, whose writings on the differences between instrumental and communicative rationality and his consensus theory of truth (Habermas, 1981) all came in handy, so to speak.

And to my delight, at my first adult education conference as a graduate student I encountered Jack Mezirow, who also had read Habermas, making me more willing to enter the adult education profession.

Turning the Economy on Its Feet

Toward the end of my graduate student days I had also started to weave feminist critiques of neocolonialism and neoliberalism into my thinking. My younger sister was then studying sociology in Germany and kept referring me to the writings of Claudia von Werlhof, one of her professors. Von Werlhof had been doing fieldwork in the 1970s in Venezuela, and her writings focused on the fate of peasants under the growing influence of neoliberalism, which by that time had been set in motion. Patriarchal–capitalist global economic developments had already started to turn subsistence work on the land into paid labor for agricultural, monocultural enterprises. While peasant men became paid laborers, peasant women were being forced into a privatized, dependent housewife existence (von Werlhof, 1985).

These feminist political–economic writings examined how and why still-existing subsistence economies in so-called Third World countries were being destroyed in the name of progress and development, a notion fully shared by leftist and mainstream political–economic theorists. Both strands of theories branded subsistence economies as either "undeveloped" or "precapitalist." Although they used different terms, both were also in agreement that these economies had to become integral components of a profit-driven private economy or a full-fledged commodity production where all activities have been transformed into an abstract, sellable labor force.

The title of one of von Werlhof's essays is indicative of what she does in all her writings: "Women and Third World as 'Nature' to Capital or the Economy Put on Its Feet" (1998). By unburying the reality that lies underneath supports, makes possible paid labor and commodity production, she therefore provides a powerful critical lens for understanding why a developed, profit-oriented capitalist patriarchy has to exploit and kill life, whereas an orientation that acknowledges and respects life sustains, nourishing it in all its forms.

I started to incorporate analyses of subsistence labor and subsistence production into my thinking and writing (Hart, 1992). I also saw how raising or working with children in the racially and economically segregated ghetto of a big city gives a prime example of the way that patriarchal, racist, and neoliberal economic processes all interlock to undermine or rip up basic conditions for doing this complex, life-affirming kind of subsistence labor (Hart, 2002).

The World of Community Organizing

About 6 years ago I was asked by *Mujeres Latinas en Acción*, a local community group, to investigate the labor conditions of Latina immigrant domestic workers in Chicago (see Hart, 2010). One of its members knew about my academic writings on subsistence work and motherwork. I started my investigation by contacting a number of community and labor or immigrant advocacy groups, but none had any programs or specific efforts in place regarding domestic workers. I clearly had to talk to the workers themselves and hear their stories.

I learned Spanish and went to parks where nannies always come with the children in their charge. I also talked to other domestic workers in community centers or at gatherings in a private household. In the process I also became a member of a Latina workers' collective that had been organized by a nanny from Columbia.

We regularly met, often in private homes due to the lack of open and friendly political spaces. Whenever the women met they brought food. One of the workers in her late 50s, troubled by arthritis and living in the far south side, always brought a major dish, hauling a big bag to a bus station, to a train station, and then from the station to our meeting place.

We were always sitting in a circle, eating, talking, or—like me—mainly listening, trying to understand. This reminded me of the 1960s and early 1970s when I participated in women's groups, but in a student environment. The members of the collective were working in hard, ill-paid jobs, took care of their families in addition to working full-time, or were unemployed because they left their jobs due to suffering abuse. Their livelihood depended on their husbands' income. They suffered abuse not only on their jobs but also in their own home. They had little or no recourse.

I was the only non-Latina, and I could barely speak their language. And yet I was always greeted with respect, always included in the conversation. The women welcomed my presence, smiled at me, allowed me to try to say something, listened carefully, and responded clearly and kindly.

In my academic world, meeting and discussing issues related to gender injustice has always been quite different. Academic women get together in an environment that is soaked in issues of power and in institutional expectations that foster habits of always being on guard; of strategizing about how to present oneself, whom to pay attention to, and with whom it is important to speak. Any discussion of radical politics is therefore not immune to a middle-class academic behavior in the form of a defensive, calculating ego-centeredness, clearly fed by the academic logic of automatic ranking and de/legitimizing.

In 2007, about a year into my efforts, the National Domestic Workers Alliance (NDWA) was formed. The Alliance is part of an emerging national and international political movement to gain respect and recognition of the importance of domestic work. In 2010 New York passed the Domestic Workers Bill of Rights, and in June 2011 the International Labor Office in Geneva adopted the First Convention and accompanying Recommendation on Decent Work for Domestic Workers, signed by over 350 governments (Committee on Domestic Workers, 2011). Events such as these not only undo the invisibility of an entire working population but also break through the entrenched patriarchal devaluing of household labor as not real work. The International Labor Office convention emphasized that on a global level

New Directions for Adult and Continuing Education • DOI: 10.1002/ace

the work of cleaning houses and caring for children, the elderly, and the disabled is of vital importance; it deserves the same legal protection as any other kind of work.

Traveling Across Divisions

When the workers' collective became a member of NDWA we were invited to participate in a national survey of domestic workers (Burnham & Theodore, 2012). We joined a local community organization, and at the end of the project decided to form the multinational, multiethnic, and multicolored Coalition of Household Workers.

Forming a strong base of household workers and their allies requires that everyone involved constantly travel across a multitude of racial–ethnic, cultural, and class divisions. The three worker leaders of the Coalition's base-building and organizing efforts are Latina, African American, and Filipina. They often display rather striking differences in terms of communication style, ways of dealing with conflict, and reaching out to other workers, causing a number of misunderstandings. Ensuing feelings of distrust are only compounded by the workers' unique stories of being inside/out the social norms in terms of color, language, country of origin, or immigration status. We are clearly in need of carefully developing what Cricket Keating describes in *Building Coalitional Consciousness* (2005) in order to build community among the workers themselves.

There are additional, related but also distinct challenges with regard to collation-building when the workers come together with others in order to form a strategic alliance around a specific goal. This was brought home to me when members of the Coalition came together with union representatives, an attorney from a labor advocacy group, and leaders from other community organizations in order to plan a public event on the rights of homecare workers. After the meeting one of workers pulled me aside and complained that "this was so academic, they talked and talked and left no space for asking any questions about things we want to understand. Were they just talking to each other?" (Anonymous, personal communication, October 26, 2012).

The worker was clearly upset about how people present at the meeting made themselves noticed, or exuded their strength in a way that illustrated that the workers had no voice in the minds of those claiming to be allies. They had no voice because several of the circuits Aimee Carrillo Rowe (2008, p. 2) refers to as "power lines" were running at full speed, above all the patriarchal power line. During all my years of working with a number of different labor or community organizations, the patriarchal power line seems to be the hardest to discern and acknowledge, let go of, or connect with those of affirmation and validation.

Rowe (2008) defines power lines as "conduits of the unevenness of modernity" that were created by centuries of colonial and neocolonial conquest and oppression (p. 2). Power lines therefore internally and externally

New Directions for Adult and Continuing Education • DOI: 10.1002/ace

crisscross all political efforts, whether performed in the name of one's particular group or organization, or in alliance with others in the pursuit of a specific goal. Where patriarchal power lines crisscross with other power lines, those excluded from them have to develop their voice, speak loudly, and claim their rights. Only then will they keep reminding their allies that they have to unlearn their patriarchal–professional sense of power and expertise, question the source of their taken-for-granted privileges, and open a space for not only strategically addressing issues related to household labor, but also for validating the workers themselves as the true experts on what rights they need or deserve.

Subverting the Logic of Higher Education

In my political work I walk the streets, and in my academic work I do "streetwalker theorizing." According to Lugones (2003, p. 224), "The streetwalker theorist cultivates a multiplicity and depth of perception and connection and 'hangs out' even in well-defined institutional spaces, troubling and subverting their logics, their intent." Above all, "Streetwalker theorizing . . . is sustained in the midst of the concrete" (p. 224).

The "concrete" that sustains my theorizing involves listening to the workers, remembering the tremendous amount of knowledge and skills my mother enacted in our daily survival struggles, and writing about the itineraries of immigrant domestic workers to and from their own homes and the home–workplace in the house of a stranger (Hart, 2013). All this has been sharpening my ears and eyes for hearing and seeing many shades and strands of a complexly woven fabric called domestic work. It has also given me training in continuously moving in between spaces intellectually, mentally, and spiritually.

I work in an alternative liberal arts undergraduate program for adult students. By being interdisciplinary, individualized, and open for welcoming experiential learning the program allows me to enact my streetwalker approach in my pedagogical practices.

Borrowing from Lugones's descriptions, as a streetwalker theorist I have been cultivating "an ear and tongue for multiple lines of meaning" (2003, p. 224). Knowing and creating knowledge are therefore dialogic processes that are always in motion. I therefore accompany my students in their learning journey by helping them discern and articulate their unique framework of sense and sense-making, and by guiding them in the development of their own theoretical understanding of the multiple and complex forms of knowledge woven into the concrete of their life and work experiences.

I consider it irrelevant how or in what form they present their theories. On one level, and in Lugones's words, as an academic–political streetwalking educator I thereby "trouble" and "subvert" the logic of a "well-defined institutional space" by encouraging students to express "different world(s) of sense that are not countenanced by institutionalized, dominant, 'official' sense"

(Lugones, 2003, p. 224). Students' expressions of their worlds of sense can come in the form of a story, an analytical essay, an artistic production, or any combination thereof. They do, however, in their own way have to illustrate that their creators have arrived at a deeper understanding of what shapes and governs the concrete of their lives, their ordinary problems, their dreams.

In a way, I am "queering the academy," as Elana Michelson so vividly describes in *Inside/Out: A Meditation on Cross-Dressing and Prior Learning Assessment* (2012). In this essay she lays bare how prior learning assessment disrupts the official and rigid boundaries between categories of knowledge because it accredits experiential learning gained through ordinary human activity. While Michelson describes how this form of "epistemological cross-dressing" (p. 6) is rather disturbing to some members of higher education, she also criticizes that prior learning assessment does not really do away with any rigid boundaries. Rather, it claims to raise "the embodied, personal, local, and at times even visceral experiential learning" to the heights of true, meaning "disembodied, universalized, idealized knowledge whose presumed purview is the academy" (p. 3). She emphasizes that it would take a much more radical undermining of the categorical distinctions to challenge this normalizing practice of prior learning assessment.

To create an open and fluid space in between the rigidly defined, interlocking fragments of officially fenced-in or walled-off worlds is one of my main pedagogical goals. It is the space where I guide students to experience the multiplicity and plurality of identity, and to discover the interstices between relations of power and the points of crisscrossing worlds and power lines. Because the classroom can be welcomed as a momentary safe learning space, I allow students to travel to each other's worlds by looking at the expressions of their sense-making, seeing how their worlds diverge, overlap, or define each other in power-bound ways. They are guided to take some first steps toward what Lugones calls "playful 'world'-traveling" where people unlearn the deeply entrenched practice of "arrogant perception" but rather start looking at the other world(s) more lovingly (2003, p. 78).

Coming to Closure

Recently I had one of those transformative learning experiences of sudden insight when going for acupuncture treatment. This insight made me embrace, and explore, the image of the circle in which the yin and the yang move into each other, with each carrying the other in a small circle inserted into their own world.

When the Korean acupuncturist asked me what I knew about the yin-yang theory, I said I did not really know anything about it, but I can sort of relate to it because for me it depicts my always living or moving in between extremes. And I emphasized that I just haven't been able to create some kind of equilibrium between any of these extremes.

His response was, "Only death brings that kind of equilibrium. When alive what you call extremes are working with, against, or for each other, are always in motion, never stand still" (Sung Choi, personal communication, December 13, 2012).

Now I understood. And that's how I see the two worlds—the world of political organizing and the world of academe—and how moving in and out of them is exhausting and exhilarating, annoying and life-giving. How they sometimes work against each other, one world shrinking while the other is taking over, and how that makes the one taking over unpleasant, or unbearable, leaving the one having shrunk unnourished and in pain. What helps me move it back to life is the inner circle that contains the essential belongings of the other world I never fully leave behind, always carry with me, drawing yin strength for moving in the yang, or yang strength for moving in the yin. Both are tucked into my backpack. Both are always in motion.

References

Braidotti, R. (1994). *Nomadic subjects: Embodiment and sexual difference in contemporary feminist theory.* New York, NY: Columbia University Press.

Burnham, L., & Theodore, N. (2012). *Home economics: The invisible and unregulated world of domestic work.* New York, NY: National Domestic Workers Alliance.

Committee on Domestic Workers. (2011, June). *Fourth item on the agenda: Decent work for domestic workers.* Report of the Committee on Domestic Workers, Provisional Record 15, from 110th Session of the International Labour Conference. Retrieved from http://www .ilo.org/wcmsp5/groups/public/@ed_norm/@relconf/documents/meetingdocument /wcms_157696.pdf

Habermas, J. (1981). *Theorie des kommunikativen Handelns* [Theory of communicative reasoning]. Frankfurt am Main, Germany: Suhrkamp.

Hart, M. (1987). *Towards a theory of collective learning* (Unpublished doctoral dissertation). Indiana University, Bloomington, IN.

Hart, M. (1992). *Working and educating for life: Feminist and international perspectives on adult education.* New York, NY: Routledge.

Hart, M. (2002). *The poverty of life-affirming work: Motherwork, education, and social change.* Westport, CT: Greenwood Press.

Hart, M. (2010). *Latinas and domestic caring work.* Unpublished manuscript, Commissioned by Mujeres Latinas en Acción, Chicago, IL.

Hart, M. (2013). Laboring and hanging out in the embodied in-between. *Hypatia, 28,* 49–86.

Jordan, J. (2005). I must become a menace. In J. H. Levi & S. Miles (Eds.), *Directed by desire: The collected poems of June Jordan* (p. 170). Port Townsend, WA: Copper Canyon Press.

Keating, C. (2005). Building coalitional consciousness. *National Women's Studies Association Journal, 17,* 86–103.

Lugones, M. (2003). *Pilgrimages/peregrinajes: Theorizing coalition against multiple oppressions.* Lanham, MD: Rowman & Littlefield.

Michelson, E. (2012). Inside/out: A meditation on cross-dressing and prior learning assessment. *PLAIO: Prior Learning Assessment Inside Out, 1*(1). Retrieved from http://www.plaio .org/index.php/home/article/view/15

Rowe, A. C. (2008). *Power lines: On the subject of feminist alliances.* Durham, NY: Duke University Press.

New Directions for Adult and Continuing Education • DOI: 10.1002/ace

von Werlhof, C. (1985). *Wenn die Bauern wiederkommen: Frauen, Arbeit und Agrobusiness in Venezuela* [When the peasants return: Women, work, and agribusiness in Venezuela]. Bremen, Germany: Edition CON.

von Werlhof, C. (1998). Frauen und Dritte Welt als "Natur" des Kapitals, oder: Ökonomie auf die Füsse gestellt [Women and Third World as "nature" to capital or the economy put on its feet]. In H. Dauber & W. Simpfendörfer (Eds.), *Eigener Haushalt und bewohnter Erdkreis. Ökologisches und ökumenisches Lernen in der "Einen Welt"* [One's own household and a lived-in planet earth: Ecologcial and economic learning in the "One World"] (pp. 187–214). Wuppertal, Germany: Peter Hammer.

MECHTHILD HART *is a professor at the School for New Learning, DePaul University, Chicago.*

New Directions for Adult and Continuing Education • DOI: 10.1002/ace

7

Labor studies can play a unique role in today's increasingly corporatized higher education.

Labor Studies: Redefining a College Education

Sharon Szymanski, Richard Wells

College does not always help you. It does not guarantee you the job that you want, or even a good paying one. Why spend thousands of dollars (on college tuition) when you could be working and making thousands instead?

Student, The Harry Van Arsdale Jr. Center for Labor Studies
(personal communication, March 7, 2012)

There are many fields of work and labor that don't require a four year education. This however doesn't mean that some sort of education beyond high school isn't necessary. For starters, even manual labor is better performed with an education behind it, but it goes further than that. It is important to have an understanding of the world around you. Not having a thorough education sets you at a disadvantage against everyone else because education is important to defend yourself politically and socially.

Student, The Harry Van Arsdale Jr. Center for Labor Studies
(personal communication, March 7, 2012)

For me college is a way to do the critical thinking I'll need to accomplish moving my family out of poverty.

Student, The Harry Van Arsdale Jr. Center for Labor Studies
(personal communication, March 7, 2012)

The above comments were written by our students, all members of a New York City–based building trade union, in response to a statement made by former Pennsylvania Senator Rick Santorum during the recent Republican

NEW DIRECTIONS FOR ADULT AND CONTINUING EDUCATION, no. 139, Fall 2013 © 2013 Wiley Periodicals, Inc.
Published online in Wiley Online Library (wileyonlinelibrary.com) • DOI: 10.1002/ace.20065

presidential primary. If you remember, Santorum dismissed President Barack Obama's goal to make higher education accessible to all. That aspiration, Santorum said, amounted to snobbery because it assumed that everyone desired and needed a college degree. As represented by Santorum's attack, today the debate about the value of a college education increasingly has been reduced to a market-based calculation. And as the words of the first student quoted above attest, this especially may be the case for working-class college students. Does it pay for someone who will be a mechanic, a home health-care aide, a plumber, an electrician, or any number of service sector and trades jobs to go deep into debt for a degree when the job they are seeking, or perhaps already have, doesn't require it?

Indeed, in today's hypermarketized society, college is often viewed as an individual investment—just like investing in stocks or bonds. If the expected *return* isn't realized (no job or no degree required for the job) then you have wasted your time and your money. These are concerns that are very real not only for our trade-union-based students (electricians, paraprofessionals, carpenters, and plumbers) but for the many recent graduates who are not able to secure jobs at all, much less jobs commensurate with their degrees. Questioning the purpose of a college education is fair game, and so far universities themselves seem to be avoiding real answers, offering up technological fixes to problems that extend well beyond the university itself and that require concentrated public debate and determined public action to address. The words of the second and third of our students, as stated in the opening quotes, suggest that this is where labor studies can play a unique role. In its content and overall purpose, labor studies is about empowerment as much as it is about job placement.

We are full-time faculty at The Harry Van Arsdale Jr. Center for Labor Studies located in New York City, a unique program within the spectrum of adult education. In September 1977, under the leadership of business manager Harry Van Arsdale Jr., Local 3 of the International Brotherhood of Electrical Workers, mandated that a college degree must be an integral component of the apprenticeship training program. This was a bold and unprecedented action, and Local 3 remains one of only a few trade unions that require a college degree as a condition of apprenticeship employment and journeyman status. It also resulted in the establishment of a Labor College within Empire State College/State University of New York, itself an institution founded on the progressive notion that working adults and other "nontraditional" students should be given access to a college education. So, while the Labor Center is actively involved in the training program of Local 3 apprentices, at the same time it performs its work inside the educational parameters and strictures of Empire State College.

Along with our students, we try to accomplish two things. On one hand, we offer some of the "tool" courses that characterize most standard labor education programs. These offerings—on the practice of collective bargaining and labor law, to take two examples—have a critical role in that they prepare future leaders for the complex job of administering a union, representing it in negotiations with management and looking out for the interests not only of members but of the labor movement as a whole. On the other hand, we also offer courses that are designed to see through the hype and misinformation that often passes for commonsense thinking about how an economy should work, how wages are determined, how politics should be conducted, how cities are planned, how the entrenched inequalities that characterize our society are understood, and how the wide range of human experience is measured and valued. This latter emphasis is on the transformational, on the building of the collective confidence to reframe in historical, sociological, and humanistic terms our view of the world so as to read it not only as it is, but as it might be (Fraser, Merrill, Ramdeholl, Szymanski, & Wells, 2011; Freire, 1970). In other words, we are trying to shift the conversation as to why "college pays."

Critical engagement in the issues of the day and the formulation of alternative visions and programs have been at the heart of working-class educational efforts in the United States (and in the United Kingdom) since the early 20th century, regardless of whether these efforts were led by voluntary associations, trade unions, universities, or some combination thereof. In this sense, worker or labor education has always been a "decentering" project, always at some level about the recognition of an experience and the political embodiment of a knowledge that had the potential to disrupt dominant narratives and help write new ones. As such it is a part of a progressive and inherently political tradition in adult education that has sought not only to provide access to an education to those who otherwise would not have it, but to democratize education in practice and to work together with other community groups and institutions such as trade unions to promote a more just and democratic culture.

This intermingling of two very established institutions—the trade union movement and the university system—presents both difficulties and possibilities for labor studies. In this article we will explore the tensions that, given their built-in public/political imperatives, have over time characterized educational programs that serve unionized workers and the working class more generally. We also will examine how, in the hostile environment in which the labor movement in the United States now operates, these tensions have led to an active debate over just what education in a labor context is and what it should do. The relationship our program has with both unions and a large state university presents limits and structures what we can do. But we will also argue that together they present opportunities to reinvent and reclaim a university education as a public good rather than a private privilege.

Situating Labor Studies Historically and Politically

Since formalized programs for worker education were first established in the early 20th century, they have had two basic imperatives. The first was to provide "nuts and bolts" practical training in the operation of the union, in terms of its relations both with members and with employers. Second was a general liberal-arts education designed to produce a politically engaged, working-class perspective on the issues and problems of the day.

During the 1920s heyday of the independent labor college the more broad-based political kind of education was stressed. As historians of the movement have shown, the organizers of labor colleges across the country sought actively to redefine a college education so that it suited the purposes of a working-class-led struggle for change (Altenbaugh, 1983, 1990; Dwyer, 1977; Tarlau, 2011). At the time, college was not only beyond the reach of the working class, but the standard curricula gave little consideration to the place of organized labor in society. But at institutions like the Brookwood Labor College, founded in Katonah, New York, in 1921, a college education meant a sharpening of the collective intellect and political acumen of a legitimate and socially necessary force: the labor movement. Worker education, in other words, was not about learning one's way out of the working class, or solely about prepping labor leaders to maintain a working relationship with management. It was about empowerment, about preparing labor to take a leading role in making a more equitable society. More modestly, it was about creating an effective and sustainable working-class *voice* in the public sphere.

Between 1924 and 1927 some 60 labor colleges were founded across the United States, and for a time it seemed a new educational day was dawning. But the socialist inclinations of many who led the fight for worker education led to stiff opposition to the labor colleges as a political movement, both from without and within the broader labor movement (Barrow, 1990). The biggest challenge, however, was financial. Most labor colleges depended heavily on support from private individuals or foundations. With the coming of the Depression, much of this support dried up, putting an end to the experiment (Altenbaugh, 1983, p. 406).

But as the federal government responded to the crisis with the programs of the New Deal, educational efforts geared toward working-class adults quickly gained new importance. Of all New Deal legislation, it was the National Labor Relations Act of 1935 (The Wagner Act) that had the most direct impact. The Act gave the labor movement formal political legitimacy by stating that workers had the right to join unions, and it protected workers from unfair labor practices. The Act also helped to spur the dramatic surge in unionization heralded by the advent of the Congress of Industrial Organizations. With a new legal environment to interpret and the tactics of collective bargaining to master, there was an immediate demand for educational programs that would train union members and leaders how to navigate the brave new world of industrial relations. Thus emerged what one historian called a "utilitarian labor education," and it was critical not simply in terms of union growth. It became "an imperative for survival" (Dwyer, 1977, p. 188). It was not until the late 1960s, with the campus-based demands for programs in women's, Black, and/or ethnic studies that labor studies emerged as a credit-bearing discipline leading to a degree.

New Directions for Adult and Continuing Education • DOI: 10.1002/ace

Today the political stakes both for organized labor itself and labor education programs are quite high. Since the early 1970s, the New Deal policies that shored up the labor movement's power have been steadily dismantled. In mainstream political discourse, unions are seen at best as relics of a bygone industrial age and at worst as obstacles to the kinds of change it is presumed will secure a future for us all. Republican governors challenge the legitimacy of collective bargaining for public workers. In the private sector, managers routinely fire workers struggling to organize workers, with little or no penalty from a now toothless National Labor Relations Board. A multimillion-dollar "Union Avoidance Industry" works full-time cutting off organizing drives before they begin and then intimidates the workers who dare talk union (Logan, 2006). Meantime, union density continues its steady decline. In the late 1940s almost one third of the workforce was in a union; today only 11.8% overall of workers are organized. Only 6.9% of private sector workers are in unions.

Of course union jobs have higher wages, benefits, better working conditions, and job security. But studies also show that unions reduce income inequality for nonunion workers as well. Until 1973, for example, union strength insured that labor productivity and wages grew together, and the standard of living increased for the majority. Wages have since lagged well behind increases in productivity, a trend that has contributed significantly to the stark income inequality that characterizes the U.S. political economy today. Without a strong labor movement, there cannot be stability and security for wage earners across the board (U.S. Senate, S. Hrg. 111–702, 2009). Indeed, one study estimates that the decline of organized labor accounts for up to one third of the rise in economic inequality in the United States over the last 30 years (Western & Rosenfeld, 2011).

In this context, union-based education programs and university-based labor studies programs are debating how best to confront both the political assault on unions and the economic onslaught on working Americans. Some university programs are turning away from nuts-and-bolts labor education, and more toward independent strategic research into local labor markets and local power structures. As the director of one program put it, "Students are less interested in the AFL [American Federation of Labor], and more in sweatshops" (Bacon, 2003). In other words, while labor studies programs today have adapted the older imperative of worker education to a new set of political-economic circumstances and to the new demographics of the working class in the United States, they are still striving to provide students with a clear sense of the political and economic context in which workers' struggles are currently taking place. Furthermore, they are providing space for students to draw out the values that have brought the struggle forward and to develop the confidence to keep it going, all the while remaining aware of the fact they are vulnerable to attack by opportunistic players on the political right.

For their part, union-based education programs are fighting to adapt to current crisis conditions in the labor movement as a whole. There is an emerging consensus among union leaders and activists that in the face of the onslaught on labor a shift in basic strategy is necessary, one that moves efforts away from what has been called a "business-service unionism" to a "social movement unionism" that places more emphasis on organizing new members, taking direct action, and raising the profile of the labor movement as an effective advocate for working men and women. As Rebecca Tarlau has documented, this shift has ignited considerable debate within labor education circles about what kind of education is needed to, so to speak, put movement back in the labor movement (Tarlau, 2011, pp. 367–368). Many activists and organizers in the labor movement have been strongly influenced by Saul Alinsky, the Chicago-based community organizer who stressed that education, or at least the education that mattered the most in the struggle for change, happened as working people organized and took action to make that change happen. In current conditions, where time is short because every day seems to bring another attack on collective bargaining and on organizing drives, Alinsky's notion that "action" spontaneously educates workers is certainly compelling.

But what happens once the goal is met, or for that matter once it is not met? Others in the field of labor education think more in the tradition of Myles Horton and Paulo Friere: Education is a more deliberate process of consciousness-raising that ideally should not simply take place during the process of organizing, but should take place before, during, *and* after. This kind of education could, moreover, make organization more effective, more legitimate in the eyes of the organized, and more sustainable over time. It was about, in Horton's words, "developing people, helping them grow, helping them become able to analyze" (Horton & Friere, 1990, p. 116).

The idea that workers need to take the time to "reread" and "rewrite" their world so that they can then remake it is a tough sell these days. Unions have cut back on internal educational programs, instead devoting precious resources to organizing and political mobilization. Many in the labor movement believe in problem posing education. But building the capacity for a longer-term educational effort is hard even when the theoretical and philosophical commitment to do so is there. As one labor leader put it, "Unions are to a large extent about alleviating pain, and the pain has to be alleviated at the moment and the fire has to be put out at the moment" (Tarlau, 2011, p. 377).

Labor Studies and the Occupy Moment

As noted above, we work within an established state university system, with all the curricular standards, requirements, and parameters that go with it. But because our students are apprentices who come to us directly through our trade union partners, we have been able to structure our program in a way that centers on both our students' life experiences and the full range of issues and themes that shape and are shaped by the labor "presence" in the economy, in the political realm, and in the wider culture. And critically, in terms of

New Directions for Adult and Continuing Education • DOI: 10.1002/ace

pedagogy, we see ourselves as popular educators, inspired by the tradition of the Labor Colleges of the 1920s and 1930s, the work of Horton and Friere (1990), and our own experience in labor education outside university settings.

Precisely because we approach our work this way, the Occupy Wall Street movement, which garnered international attention in the fall of 2011, crystallized in our own minds what our work is all about. In addition to it being a remarkable moment of organization and political resistance, it was also a significant *educational* moment. It publicized the alarming gap between the rich and the rest in the United States. It spurred important conversations in public spaces and on the airwaves about tax policy; about the ongoing financialization of our economy; and about the triple whammy of skyrocketing tuition, student debt, and the ever-shrinking supply of decent jobs with decent pay and benefits for those getting out of college. Occupy's persistent broadcasting of the fact that the top 1% of Americans has a greater net worth than the entire bottom 90% turned what had been a statistic discussed for the most part only in economics departments into a figure of popular discourse. Indeed, even for people who didn't agree with the tactics of Occupy activists, the topics of the dismal science became less dismal. Furthermore, the notion of "fairness" in relation to wealth, taxes, jobs, access to education, and health care spilled out of the rarified spaces of college philosophy, ethics, law, literature, and economic courses into debates in *public* spaces, taking its rightful place as a defining theme of civic life.

Occupy reminded us of two related impulses behind our efforts. For one, loudly and clearly, it proclaimed that the kinds of themes we explore throughout our curriculum at the Van Arsdale Center—that the inequality we now face is not inevitable, but the result of the bad ideas and the bad policy spawned by the dominance of neoliberalism; that unionists and working men and women must join together and read and rewrite the world from their own perspective; and that a more just society can be imagined, and therefore is possible—are themes held in common by many outside the confines of our labor center. We often stress at orientations and in our classes that labor must tell its own story. Others have been writing that script for too long and at great social cost. By shifting the larger political debate Occupy made it clear that working men and women had to tell that story not only to themselves, but to the public at large.

But more generally, Occupy's capturing of the public imagination by its hard focus on issues that affect the majority reminded us of an important way in which we differ from mainstream colleges in general, beyond the fact that our students are "nontraditional." A college education, by and large, has become a kind of private transaction: The college provides the degree in exchange for a fee, the expectation being that the receiver of the degree will then have some individual advantage, primarily in the job market. The purpose of college, in other words, is to serve as a ladder for social mobility that students climb one at a time, and college administrations the country overspend their marketing dollars to promote their accomplishments in this

New Directions for Adult and Continuing Education • DOI: 10.1002/ace

regard. Yet as many Occupy activists insisted, this particular logic is not grounded in current reality. Today one half of the graduates of the college class of 2012 are either jobless or underemployed (in jobs that don't utilize their knowledge and skills), suggesting to some that in an economic sense a degree doesn't pay off, given high tuition and the burden of student loans (Weissmann, 2012). Furthermore, even when low-income, working-class students do everything by the book in terms of preparing themselves academically, the demands of college-level work and being away from family produce economic and social strains that are difficult to overcome (De Parle, 2012).

Indeed, our students' own experiences offer a strong critique of the value of college education, at least when that value is tied to the notion of the college as a job ladder. But labor studies is different; it is an education with a different kind of value, one geared toward the building of collective consciousness and power. In other words, like the labor colleges of old, a degree in labor studies must afford not social mobility but *political mobility* for what the economist Michael Zweig has referred to as the working-class majority (Zweig, 2000). It is not about getting an education so that one can rise out of one's class. It is about getting the education that helps the working class build the kind of labor movement that will give itself an equal voice in a public sphere that has for too long been dominated by corporate interests. A labor-studies-focused college education creates scholarship that enables students to analyze the issues of the day and inspires them to take the lead in exploring alternative positions and policies. It is, to borrow the language of Ernest Boyer, one-time chancellor of the State University of New York, a "staging ground" for public action (Fraser et al., 2011).

As we see it, there is nothing more or less "political" about giving this kind of purpose to an academic program in labor studies than there is in the "purpose" of a degree in business administration or marketing. As Elaine Bernard, executive director of the Labor and Worklife program at Harvard Law School, said, "Can you imagine a business administrative program that doesn't take for granted the need to make profits or that doesn't want to talk to business leaders, or place its students in companies" (Bacon, 2003)? However, one of our fundamental laws acknowledges that employees, not just employers, have legitimate and critical roles to play in sustaining economic activity. The Preamble to the 1935 National Labor Relations Act states that workers *should*, for the benefit of the economy and the society as a whole, "have full freedom of association, self-organization, and designation of representatives of their own choosing, for the purpose of negotiating the terms and conditions of their employment or other mutual aid or protection."

While few in corporate America these days take this idea seriously, for us it is a basic point of departure. Indeed, there is no historical grounding, or for that matter ethical grounding, for the idea that profit-taking is the be-all and end-all of an economy, even one that relies on markets. Simply put, labor matters and its perspective on the world matters, more than ever before.

At a time when universities are redefining their mission in the face of budget cuts and pressure from corporate-minded "innovators" that populate boards of trustees—witness the recent turmoil at the University of Virginia (Rice, 2012)—perhaps labor studies is a bit of a throwback. The president of Wesleyan University, Michael S. Roth, recently urged us in *The New York Times* to recall the refrain of John Dewey, who argued that practical training was surely necessary, but an education that merely adapted a student to the existing economic system—generated "human capital" in today's parlance—was a bad idea given all the profound injustices generated by that system. "In a nation that aspires to Democracy," writes Roth, education is primarily about "the cultivation of freedom in society" (Roth, 2012). We very much agree with the sentiment, although we are inclined to add some urgency to it. As expressed by the student in the second quote introducing this article, you need an education "to defend yourself politically and socially."

References

Altenbaugh, R. J. (1983). The children and instruments of a militant labor progressivism: Brookwood Labor College and the American labor college movement of the 1920s and 1930s. *History of Education Quarterly, 23*, 395–411.

Altenbaugh, R. J. (1990). *Education for struggle: The American labor colleges of the 1920s and 1930s.* Philadelphia, PA: Temple University Press.

Bacon, D. (2003, December). Class warfare. *The Nation.* Retrieved from http://www.thenation.com/article/class-warfare-0

Barrow, C. W. (1990). Counter-movement within the labor movement: Workers' education and the American Federation of Labor, 1900–1937. *Social Science Journal, 27*(4), 395–418.

DeParle, J. (2012, December 22). For poor, leap to college often ends in a hard fall. *The New York Times.* Retrieved from http://www.nytimes.com/2012/12/23/education/poor-students-struggle-as-class-plays-a-greater-role-in-success.html?pagewanted=all&_r=0

Dwyer, R. (1977). Workers' education, labor education, labor studies: An historical delineation. *Review of Educational Research, 47*(1), 179–207.

Fraser, R., Merrill, M., Ramdeholl, D., Szymanksi, S., & Wells, R. (2011). The Van Arsdale Center: A staging ground for action. In D. Amory, L. Matthews, E. Michelson, M. C. Powers, & S. Szymanski (Eds.), *Revisiting Boyer: Exploring the scholarly work of Empire State College faculty* (pp. 47–51). Saratoga Springs, NY: SUNY Empire State College.

Freire, P. (1970). *Pedagogy of the oppressed.* New York, NY: Seabury Press.

Horton, M., & Freire, P. (1990). In B. Bell, J. Gaventa, & J. Peters (Eds.), *We make the road by walking: Conversations on education and social change.* Philadelphia, PA: Temple University Press.

Logan, J. (2006). The union avoidance industry in the United States. *British Journal of Industrial Relations, 44*(4), 651–675.

National Labor Relations Act, Pub. L. No. 74-198, 29 U.S.C. § 151–169, 49 Stat. 449 (1935).

Rice, A. (2012, September 11). Anatomy of a campus coup. *The New York Times.* Retrieved from http://www.nytimes.com/2012/09/16/magazine/teresa-sullivan-uva-ouster.html?pagewanted=all

Roth, M. S. (2012, September 5). Learning as freedom. *The New York Times.* Retrieved from http://www.nytimes.com/2012/09/06/opinion/john-deweys-vision-of-learning-as-freedom.html

Tarlau, R. (2011). Education and labor in tension: Contemporary debates about education in the US labor movement. *Labor Studies Journal, 36*(3), 363–387.

U.S. Senate, Committee on Health, Education, Labor, and Pensions. (2009). *Rebuilding economic security: Empowering workers to restore the middle class* (S. Hrg. 111–702). (Testimony of Paula Voos). Washington, DC: Government Printing Office.

Weissmann, J. (2012, April 23). 53% of recent college grads are jobless or underemployed— How? *The Atlantic*. Retrieved from http://www.theatlantic.com/business /archive/2012/04/53-of-recent-college-grads-are-jobless-or-underemployed-how/256237/

Western, B., & Rosenfeld, J. (2011). Unions, norms, and the rise in U.S. wage inequality. *American Sociological Review, 76*(4), 513–537.

Zweig, M. (2000). *The working class majority: America's best kept secret.* Ithaca, NY: ILR Press.

SHARON SZYMANSKI *is an associate professor in labor economics and political economy at the Harry Van Arsdale Jr. Center for Labor Studies, State University of New York Empire State College.*

RICHARD WELLS *is an assistant professor of anthropology and cultural history at the Harry Van Arsdale Jr. Center for Labor Studies, State University of New York Empire State College.*

New Directions for Adult and Continuing Education • DOI: 10.1002/ace

8

This chapter explores the creative ways in which WE LEARN (Women Expanding Literacy Education Action Resource Network) empowers women's full participation in community across all literacy levels.

Creating a Community of Women Educated in Literacy

Mev Miller

A Snapshot

In an archive of photographs, one snapshot may seem a bit uninteresting, just another one of many group photos. It shows six happy, smiling, clapping women and one man. Two of the women (one Black, one White) are hugging in the center while the others look on. It's obviously a "feel good" moment. Perhaps this is an award ceremony. Viewers unfamiliar with the context will likely pass over it quickly.

But when I look at the image, I remember this as a culminating moment. I know the people in the photo and the situation, so I see the layers of textures, stories, meanings, and even triumph. The people pictured include a Pakistani graduate student researching women's issues and literacy to take new learnings back to her home country. One is a tenured Latina professor of sociology and women's studies who had been a gang member. There are four White people pictured. One is a 20-something college graduate working as an administrative assistant and considering her next career move. Another is a professor of adult education. The man is a researcher and professor of literacy education. The White woman in the hug is an elder who has had a long career as a machinist, labor activist, workforce development coordinator, and career readiness specialist. The Black woman in the hug is a single mom and a middle-aging former adult literacy student pursuing a college degree. She had just

This article builds on Miller's chapter "WE LEARN: Working on Fertile Edges," first published in *Empowering Women Through Literacy: Views from Experience* (2009) by Information Age Publishing.

NEW DIRECTIONS FOR ADULT AND CONTINUING EDUCATION, no. 139, Fall 2013 © 2013 Wiley Periodicals, Inc.
Published online in Wiley Online Library (wileyonlinelibrary.com) • DOI: 10.1002/ace.20066

finished singing "Bluff is what you do when you can't read or write . . ." (Francis, 2012).

Unseen in the picture are at least another 40 to 50 women (and a few men) of various ages, professions, races, languages, nationalities, economic means, sexualities, and life experiences. This diverse gathering also includes women of varying educational levels: adult literacy and basic education learners, English language learners, college and grad students, literacy teachers, adult education professional developers, academic researchers and professors, community activists, administrators, support staff, professional women, and even a high school student. The room is the auditorium of a state university. The event is the closing ceremony of the 2010 Women Expanding Literacy Education Action Resource Network (WE LEARN) Conference.

The writer–singer of "Bluff" was not invited to an academic conference to represent the viewpoint of large numbers of literacy women needing literacy services. The Adult Basic Education (ABE), English for Speakers of Other Languages, and General Education Development (GED) learners present in the circle were not passive witnesses to an event *about* them. Rather, they made up 40% of the attendees that year and had very active roles as planners, presenters, speakers, and organizers working as adult women in a peer-to-peer context alongside teachers, advocates, administrators, activists, and university-based faculty to create a powerful women-centered event addressing issues relevant to adult literacy learners. In the field of adult basic literacy education, this event was (and continues to be) both unusual and unprecedented. That happening did not emerge overnight; it manifested a blossoming of fertile ground cultivated after years of work by dozens of volunteers and hundreds of supporters. And it provides a glimmer of what can happen when *the* central focus of an educational community is about holistic learning, respectful peer-to-peer collaboration, and shared knowledge-building rather than an exhibition of competitive academic rank.

Interlude: Introducing WE LEARN and Its Origins

WE LEARN (Women Expanding Literacy Education Action Resource Network) is a community promoting women's literacy as a tool that fosters empowerment and equity for women. Through teaching/learning events (including conferences), publications, research, special projects, and a website of resources [welearnwomen.org], WE LEARN works to provide opportunities and resources for literacy learners to engage with women-centered materials. WE LEARN increases awareness and support of women's literacy issues and assists adult literacy educators to support women's learning, especially through women-focused curriculum resources. A participatory nonprofit organization (incorporated in 2003) run completely on volunteer effort and guided by feminist/womanist principles, members of WE LEARN understand that empowering women through literacy means creating social equity and transforming our world. In this way, WE LEARN addresses the barriers

New Directions for Adult and Continuing Education • DOI: 10.1002/ace

and impact of gender-based differences on women's literacy learning and how those differences affect women's success and ability to progress socially, economically, and politically. Women-centered education means seeking and creating teaching/learning environments supported by holistic (mind, body, emotion, spirit) possibilities.

I am the founder of WE LEARN, an effort that has occupied my creative energies and organizing work for more than 15 years. WE LEARN emerged through my recognition of education and literacy as a primary key to access information, knowledge, community leadership, and power centers (Miller, 2002).

Working on a Fertile Edge

In *The Earth Path*, Starhawk (2004) asks the forest "How do systems change?" She ponders, as many activists have, whether systems can be changed from working within them or by confronting them from the outside. In the end, she takes her lead from Mary Daly who discusses working from the edges. As Starhawk puts it, "Wherever we are, we can look for those fertile edges of systems, those places where unusual niches and dynamic forces can be found, and make change there" (p. 38). WE LEARN provides learners, teachers, tutors, researchers, academics, librarians, feminist/womanist activists, professionals, and other constituents with that fertile edge and unusual niche to explore the possibilities of women's empowerment through learning that happens across a diversity of literacies and academic experience. Inspiring adult literacy learners and teachers to participate in the mission and opportunities offered by WE LEARN has been relatively easy. This is one of the very few forums to embrace their full and equal participation.

Attracting visibility and sustaining credibility across university-based academic arenas, specifically in women's studies and adult education, remain a struggle. Since our beginnings, we have consistently made efforts to speak "the language of power" to key audiences in university settings in order to make visible adult women's literacy issues in academic curriculum. Examples include the preparation of a special issue for *Women's Studies Quarterly* (Miller & Alexander, 2004), collaborated volumes published by Information Age Publishing (Miller & King, 2009, 2011), presentations and exhibits at professional conferences sponsored by women's studies and adult education organizations, participation on academic listservs (WMST-L, AAACE-NLA, professionaldevelopment@nifl, now LINCS, etc.), video posted on our website, direct snail mailings to university department chairs and professors, collaborations with internship programs, and other means. This chapter represents another foray into the tower!

One way to know if these efforts have had impact in academia might be active course adoptions of the books, but the sales numbers indicate that this has not been the case. Another way to see measurable effects would be noticeable increases in WE LEARN membership or donations from these audiences,

New Directions for Adult and Continuing Education • DOI: 10.1002/ace

attendance at WE LEARN conferences (more on this to follow), or general interest through correspondences. Overall, we have not seen such measurable results in any of these indicators. Over the years, I have learned that the impact of WE LEARN's work may not always be visible to us, so I hesitate to say our efforts have made no difference. Based on years of collected anecdotal information, I never doubt that WE LEARN's work holds relevance for and direct impact on basic literacy learners and teachers. I'm a believer in qualitative results even when the quantitative can't be verified. But in this current milieu of evidence-based practices, I would venture to say WE LEARN's work directly with the academy has netted slim results in terms of increasing the visibility of women's literacy needs and issues *within the academy*. Building collaborations with women literacy learners or making academic/feminist discourse accessible to literacy learners remains vague.

The process of building WE LEARN has always held tension of communication and expectation in relation to university-based academic theory and language, adult basic education national reporting system and workforce development guidelines, and holistic visions of women's literacy and learning needs. The change that the network creates or the successes we have may not be easily identifiable or measurable in the ways funders and educational systems demand. WE LEARN exists in a space of conundrum and contradiction. We call for an accessibility of language so that adult women with limited literacy or education can fully participate in creating solutions to the myriad of issues affecting their lives (poverty or economic stress, addiction, health, sexuality, childcare, transportation, community violence, career choice, labor rights, etc.). But adult learners want to be treated with respect as peers. That would mean using plain language without condescension or "dumbing down." This conflict of comprehension also exists for literacy teachers and community activists who are often alienated from academic circles. They too deeply understand the community socioeconomic-cultural challenges and complexities and want to participate in creating real solutions through accessible discussion. Unfortunately, elitist academic language, insistence on sometimes inflexible countable (quantitative) standardized outcomes, and obfuscation of complexities breed contempt for intelligencia and maintain the un(b)reachable ivory tower.

Our members, especially adult learners, know that more education, achievement of a GED diploma, and pursuit of a college degree will better their chances of economic stability and improve their overall quality of life. And yet, college professors who generally are still unaware of basic literacy challenges disparage arrival in college of students unable to effectively complete the academic work. Meanwhile, dedicated students often exhaust their funding for higher education while taking required college readiness courses. And yet, students and advocates outside the academy aspire to gain the social/cultural capital afforded through college and university degrees.

One reason for the existence of WE LEARN is to bridge this divide within a community, achieving women's empowerment through accessible education.

New Directions for Adult and Continuing Education • DOI: 10.1002/ace

When presenting this vision at a feminist rhetoric(s) conference in the late 1990s and experiencing some resistance, one panelist tried to come to my defense by indicating that perhaps I did not mean that feminist academics should not be doing high theory. My position silenced, I was unable to respond completely; I wanted to say that I did if it meant such theory remains decontextualized and continues to alienate and dismiss community-based discussion on real-life systemic change that benefits the daily lives of women excluded by ivory tower discourses. Over the years, the network's members have identified and successfully pursued activities that work the fertile edge to create educational/academic bridges.

Creating Spaces for Women's Learning: The (Net) Working "Un"-Conference

The active members of WE LEARN consistently reflect on what projects to pursue, their immediate impact, and how to create them as longer-term meaningful learning events. One such program is the (net)working conference, so-called because all attendees are invited and encouraged to actively participate in creating the community learning environment, that is, the *work* of WE LEARN. As this event has developed over the years, it could be understood as working a fertile edge toward the transformation of women's literacy empowerment.

In some ways, academic conferences reveal the microcosm of educational segregation. Many are an endless treadmill of panels and presentations where hopeful graduate students and academic elite talk *at* small and large audiences. In some cases, these conferences are highly competitive affairs, a chance to build one's professional portfolio (publish or perish), or an opportunity for a sponsoring organization to promote new policy. Rarely are the conferences opportunities for collaboration or furthering dialog on a common project.

The seven WE LEARN conferences held between 2004 and 2012 have been developed and planned by a dedicated group of member volunteers representing many diversities. The thematic focus for each conference has been generated by the stated needs of participants. Invited keynote speakers and panelists have been largely recruited from within our member ranks, though outside "experts" have sometimes been invited.

This event does have all the identifiable features of a conference, namely, keynote address, workshops, research presentations, panels and town halls, and a small exhibit area. But it also prioritizes many atypical characteristics in the ways we create a women-centered learning environment. The workshop presenters include ABE students as well as teachers and researchers. The topics span from practical application, participatory to reflective, and theoretical to academic. We include a designated quiet space for reflection (healing, crying, meditating, journaling, etc.). We integrate time for attention to spirit and body through activities such as yoga, ongoing art-making, music, walks, stretching and other physical activity.

New Directions for Adult and Continuing Education • DOI: 10.1002/ace

One element that I think many of us might learn from and think about was the way in which learners and practitioners participated together in many of the workshops in ways that had more to do with our commonalities as women/people and far less to do with the distinctions between our roles as learners or teachers. In part, this was because facilitators geared their workshops specifically to include all, but also because the tone of the entire conference was such that we had gathered because of a wide range of shared interests and were made to feel welcome, were listened to, and had opportunities to speak in a very receptive space. (WE LEARN, 2005)

After reading the 2006 evaluations, the conference planning work group laughingly described the WE LEARN event as an *un*-conference. The committee recognized that the typical experience or definitions of professional conference did not describe what we created; our learning/sharing space felt more like an energetic celebration gathering, festival of sorts. We continue to call it a conference, though, because the term contains the level of power and credibility needed for educators who want credit for participating in a professional development event.

To alleviate economic disparities, both nourishing and healthy breakfast and lunch are offered to all attendees as part of the registration fee. The food generally comes from community-based student-training workforce development programs. We purposefully make a sensory environment—colorful banners, fresh flowers, and other places for beauty. We include music, performance art and storytelling, and other sense-ual happenings.

One central and highlighted cornerstone of the conference is the Celebration of Student Writers. During this event, emerging writers read their stories or essays published in *Women's Perspectives*, a journal of writings by adult literacy learners produced annually by WE LEARN members. WE LEARN has published seven issues to date on a variety of themes. The power of women's voice and the opportunity for growth and empowerment expand when women are able to tell their stories in their own words. Diane Hunter wrote:

My favorite part of the WE LEARN conference was when I met a woman in the restroom. We both shared our nervousness. She said to me that she had spoken at conferences before and she should be used to it by now. It didn't dawn on me that she was someone important because I was so nervous. It just went over my head. So I told her that it was my first time speaking in front of a lot of people. We both laughed. We checked to make sure that we looked our best and then she let me know that I would speak well. I was the fifth person to read an essay out of twelve wonderful student speakers. The time came for the keynote speaker, Antonia Darder. I was so surprised when I saw Antonia; she was the lady I met in the restroom. She acknowledged me, and it made me feel good. After everything was over, people came up to me telling me how well I did. I was so overwhelmed with joy because I didn't think I did so well. Antonia

Darder came up to me and whispered to me how well I did. My whole world changed in front of my eyes. (Jones & Hunter, 2007)

With every issue of *Women's Perspectives* and with the Celebration of Student Writers, we hear stories from teachers and learners about the positive and powerful lives this experience has had on learners as they develop confidence, voice, and leadership. From this experience, learners have become active on WE LEARN committees, including the board of directors. They have traveled, prepared and presented workshops, become leaders in their communities, pursued college degrees, and taken on more advanced writing projects (one student became the regular editor of the student column in the WE LEARN newsletter).

Through the conference experience, women breathe more freely, and they (re)discover how learning can be enjoyable, fun, and playful. One of our members who has attended all the conferences commented that she does not know how we do it. She observed that she thinks it cannot get any better, but then it does.

We continue to find ways to create a participant-centered teaching/learning environment involving the whole person—mind, body, emotion, and spirit; cognitive/affective; action/reflection; basically, an atmosphere of nurturing worthiness and wellness. We are marginalized women creating our own sources for networking and support. We create a safer village of learning for a few days. The relative smallness of the conference (no more than 200 people) contributes to the comfortable community environment.

As a professor and director of adult education and Human Resource Development . . . I have found that my involvement in WE LEARN is invaluable for my personal and professional growth. . . . the most enduring aspects of WE LEARN for me are found among the collaborative, sharing relationships. It is rewarding to be part of an active community of women dedicated to sharing information and opportunities through our experiences. . . . We are celebrating and working together to help others catch a vision of their possibilities, to enable more women to climb on top of our shoulders and reach higher into their futures. (King, 2009)

We understand the critical importance of accessibility, not only in terms of literacy, but also in terms of logistical, cultural, and financial components. For example, the space location must be Americans with Disabilities Act–accessible, near public transportation (both locally and nationally) and parking. We avoid the uninviting sterile hotel setting and opt for collaborations (though our members) at local university campuses. This atmosphere also demystifies the university environment for adult learners, many of whom have never stepped on a campus. It expands their imagination to think they, too, can attend college. We try to maintain cultural accessibility as well. Members noted our earliest conferences had primarily been based on Ivy League institutions so challenged us to make connections with more genuinely community-based public institutions. We have. Curiously, one of the women's studies departments at an Ivy League school actively disassociated itself from our presence on its campus.

Cultural accessibility also refers to the ways that we embrace and reflect the many diversities of our constituents. The programming committee works to assure our speakers and presenters include learners, teachers, researchers, and administrators not only in adult basic education but also in other related activist women-centered work. Our workshops and presenters include women reflecting the broad ranges of ages, races, ethnicities, languages, sexualities, educational experience, and interests. Workshops represent a spectrum of learning styles through interaction, participation, drama, poetry, literature, movement, media, and technology.

Financial accessibility remains critical for this event. Taking into account that the accommodations and travel are costly, we have tried to keep the registration fees low. Many of our constituents are poor or low-income with limited access to funds. Cost not only affects ABE learners and graduate students, but also includes the majority of literacy practitioners who often juggle several part-time positions with no benefits in order to make ends meet. Their programs rarely have budget to support student involvement in events such as this, and the teachers receive only limited funding support for professional development. Keeping this in mind, we offer early bird discounts, discounts to presenters, and some work-exchange opportunities for part-time teachers and students. We offer registration discounts to members and have established a scholarship fund to support ABE students. Unlike many academic organizations that use their professional conferences as their primary institutional source of income, WE LEARN balances the uneasy tension between using the conference as a "fundraiser" while making it affordable and meaningful to the attendees. We have held true to a break-even bottom line in order to invite fuller participation from those often left out of educational experiences because of finances.

A women's literacy conference in itself may not appear all that radical or even movement building. However, the WE LEARN (Net)Working Conference does offer a participatory teaching/learning environment in a broad sense. Elisabeth Hayes and Daniele Flannery (2000) outline a myriad of ways in which women are learners. This research suggests that we do a disservice to women by viewing education in narrowly prescribed institutional and formal parameters. They outline a broad kaleidoscope of coexisting links for women's learning through social contexts, self-esteem and identity, voice, communication, and transformation. In most cases, this learning does not always involve print-based media or tangible curriculum standards but depends on more interactive and interpersonal motivations and contexts. These contexts provide the foundations for all of WE LEARN's programming.

New Directions for Adult and Continuing Education • DOI: 10.1002/ace

WE LEARN Empowering Women

Does WE LEARN work a fertile edge or make a difference? Do we empower women's literacy? Do we support teachers? Does our attention to the literacy needs of disenfranchised women impact systemic change? Do learners benefit from our projects? In some ways, it may be easy to romanticize our work. But then we do receive heartfelt writing from participants who do remind us of our fertile edge on the unusual niche. We can't always know the impact . . . but through the evaluations attendees have offered reflections that give us a glimpse of its revolutionary potential.

> [After I attended the 2009 conference], I had told everyone who would listen that I wanted them to experience "it" too. . . . What was the "it" that I wanted everyone to be able to share? . . . That word is PASSION. Yes, Passion is the word that best sums up my experience of WE LEARN. Passion is a life-giving self-renewing energy force. I am a passionate woman and it was my passion for laughter and healing that lead the way and gave me courage. . . . At WE LEARN I met many other passionate women. Women passionate about women and literacy! This shared passion allowed us to bond together for a weekend as equals. The conference provided an arena where passionate women honoured one another, not because of academic, social or economic standing, but because our shared passion allowed us to see the innate value within each other without needing to rely on some external measure, title or label. At different times in my life I have been at social justice events. I have heard the ideal of equality and equity spoken of and preached but until I went to the WE LEARN Conference I had never experience it lived. (Ssedoga, 2009)

One of the amazing realities about the participants connected with WE LEARN has been their commitment to feminist/womanist pedagogies and activism, their own familiarity with and connection to Freirean-based popular education, and their stances as critical knowledge-makers and colearners. WE LEARN members articulate and integrate into practice the languages of resistance and their radical/critical lenses. They embrace and live the change they want to be. We tend not to worry so much about deconstruction but rather to envision and build—from the grassroots—more holistic (mind, body, spirit, emotion) teaching/learning possibilities, thus supporting women in the broadest educational sense.

As a membership network, WE LEARN embraces the energies, expertise, and experiences of teachers, advocates, students, and community members who have seen firsthand the ways that literacy education opens a world of opportunity for women. We are all activist-scholars who continue to explore, understand, unpack, and challenge the repressive policies and curriculums that impact women learners in ABE who are generally marginalized or disenfranchised through institutionalized oppressions based on race, gender, class, violence, ethnicity, citizenship, learning disability, and other intersecting factors.

WE LEARN's work has had pendulum-type swings between the poles of a strong university-type academic and a free community of broad learning. The conference has shown us that. During the first few years, academic presenters had embraced the conference. We could tell that grad students had been encouraged to use the WE LEARN conference as a forum to practice presentation skills. In several cases, university professors (with or without colleagues) would attend only to make their presentation then leave. As the conference began to centralize more adult literacy learners and practitioner experience, many university-based presenters (especially grad students) were no longer as involved. One professor reflected that there simply was not enough academic rigor or research involved to keep the university-based participants interested. Again, we face the conundrum. For WE LEARN, a continual challenge remains: How do we assess or prove what may be more qualitative and affective rather than what can be quantifiable and cognitive? How do we remain critical and holistic when professionalism or ivory tower isolationism contradicts our vision? How do we celebrate and account for the daily, seemingly simple, accomplishments made by literacy learners (who generally do not get recognized or counted) within the powerful embrace of a women-supportive environment?

As we seek to transform women's lives through adult basic literacy education, we build an organization/movement in which constituents feel not only like they belong, but also that they can affect the organization and its direction through active participation and input. And, by extension, they can impact the larger systems of oppression that limit women's lives and possibilities as well as those of their families and communities. The key to WE LEARN's work and vision remains that we continue to mobilize a grassroots coalition building a movement to support women's literacy empowerment through collaboration and critical consciousness. We do so with women-centered visions of shared power, empowerment, joy, enjoyment, rejuvenation, and possibility. WE LEARN and we *are* the fertile places, working on the edges to weave dynamic forces for transformation and change.

References

Francis, D. (2012). *Bluff* [Video file]. Retrieved from http://www.youtube.com/watch?v=PZ kOZHe5bPk&feature=plcp

Hayes, E., & Flannery, D. D. (Eds.). (2000). *Women as learners: The significance of gender in adult learning*. San Francisco, CA: Jossey-Bass.

Jones, D., & Hunter, D. (2007, June). Don't bury those notes from conference—Use them. *WE LEARN Newsletter—News, Notes, Networking*. Retrieved from http://welearnwomen .org/files/news/07springnews.pdf

King, K. P. (2009, Fall). What I gain from my involvement with WE LEARN. *WE LEARN Newsletter—News, Notes, Networking*. Retrieved from http://welearnwomen.org/files/ news/09fallnews.pdf

Miller, M. (2002). *Women's literacy power: Collaborative approaches to developing and distributing women's literacy resources* (Doctoral dissertation). Retrieved from Proquest, UMI Dissertation Publishing. (3058540)

Miller, M., & Alexander, I. (Eds.). (2004). Women and literacy: Moving from power to participation [Special Issue]. *Women's Studies Quarterly, 32*(1–2). New York, NY: Feminist Press at CUNY.

Miller, M., & King, K. (Eds.). (2009). *Empowering women through literacy: Views from experience.* Charlotte, NC: Information Age Publishing.

Miller, M., & King, K. (Eds.). (2011). *Our stories, ourselves: The emBODYment of women's literacy.* Charlotte, NC: Information Age Publishing.

Ssedoga, K. (2009, Spring). Passionate force. *WE LEARN Newsletter—News, Notes, Networking.* Retrieved from http://welearnwomen.org/files/news/09springnews.pdf

Starhawk. (2004). *The earth path: Grounding your spirit in the rhythms of nature.* San Francisco, CA: Harper San Francisco.

WE LEARN. (2005). [Evaluation response from conference participant]. Unpublished raw data.

MEV MILLER, EdD, is the founder of WE LEARN (Women Expanding Literacy Education Action Resource Network) and currently works as the Community Resource and Hunger Study Coordinator for the Rhode Island Community Food Bank.

New Directions for Adult and Continuing Education • DOI: 10.1002/ace

9

In the concluding chapter of this volume, the author critically reflects on the important implications outlined by other authors, and through raising questions, invites us to envision and work toward a more compassionate and humane world.

What Time Is It on the Clock of the Universe?

Dianne Ramdeholl

> I think we are not conscious of the degree to which our society has moved us to see people as "others," or how we've lost the essential quality that has allowed the human race to evolve. That sense that we are each other's harvest; we are each other's business. It goes back to an epistemology, a theory of knowledge that is not just of the brain but of the heart. An epistemology of compassion that recognizes how we belong to each other, that recognizes we are each other's harvest, we are each other's business. . . . To be at that time on the clock of the universe when we can make that huge change from "othering" other people to feeling that they are part of us and we are part of them—that's a wonderful opportunity!
>
> Grace Lee Boggs—*The Next American Revolution* (2012)

I want to consider what it would mean for us, as adult educators, to decenter the notion of the academy (and all of its historical exclusionary underpinnings). To reimagine the spaces and places in which we live and where the "center" or locus of power is. I would like us, as adult educators, to ask ourselves to what extent we can all be a part of decentering in the interests of creating a more equitable, just society for all groups, as well as reorganizing society in ways that have the best interests of the majority of the people who live here (not just the very wealthy)? How can the academy (and those of us who work within these institutions) support the work and movements being fought and refought in the streets of communities?

I want to begin to ask what alternatives must exist in order to nurture more equitable political visions. To be able to reimagine ways of political

NEW DIRECTIONS FOR ADULT AND CONTINUING EDUCATION, no. 139, Fall 2013 © 2013 Wiley Periodicals, Inc.
Published online in Wiley Online Library (wileyonlinelibrary.com) • DOI: 10.1002/ace.20067

organizing that include the blurring and remaking of previous models? As Peter Marcuse (personal communication, December 1, 2012) asked, what would it be like to reimagine a society where market relations are replaced by voluntary relations? What exactly is our capacity for humanness with and for each other? If our society was reorganized in ways grounded in collective social transformation, what might our roles be as actors and agents in shaping this history, and what might the spaces of possibility that exist in which to define and develop participatory practices look like? If we were all to take the concept of Occupy Wall Street literally, what might that specifically look like? What might be other equitable uses for the buildings that define and make up Wall Street? The Stock Exchange? Chase Bank? Could we use one of those buildings as a place to provide safe spaces for vulnerable populations? To begin to engage what it would mean to redefine, reimagine, and sustain a revolution in such an advanced capitalist society would be an extraordinary challenge. Yet many, including the authors in this volume, have spent much of their lives working to support these struggles (without co-opting or colonizing them) from inside and outside the academy.

Perhaps we have reached a time when it's no longer enough to repeat what's been done in the past. Maybe we ought to focus instead on what Boggs (1998) defines as visionary organizing, the notion of not just working to develop alternative and progressive institutions that support us with "reimagining ourselves as more human human beings" (Boggs, 1998, p. 152), but also being able to clearly develop well-thought-out critiques of the current systems—well-thought-out critiques of the ways in which higher education is entrenched in and furthers the interests of these systems, and well-defined critiques of ways in which, under current dominant structures, individuals or groups are forced to be consumed with getting more for him- or herself (where almost everything we take into our bodies and minds has been transformed into a commodity).

How can we as adult educators in the academy further notions of decentering by taking part in reimagining spaces where healthy relationships with people, nature, and ourselves can be built—by creating beloved and loving communities? To what extent can visionary organizing support collective healing from capitalist dehumanization, restoring an awareness of people's innate ability to create (Birkold, 2012)?

In this volume, a broad range of practitioners and academics have discussed ways in which they've worked (and continue to) to cocreate space with the goal of exploding, reimagining, and shattering dominant "centers". . . of mapping alternative spaces within and outside the margins to further democracy and equity. This constant fluidity of outsider/insiderness and push/pull tension is eloquently described in many of the chapters as the authors navigate and negotiate terrain, sometimes discovering edges in their landscapes.

Coming from the political world of grassroots adult literacy education, one which is largely rooted in collectivity, social change, and activism, I am still unused to the ways in which academia privileges individualism and competition with deep insularity embedded within its core. Mev Miller further unpacks this tension in Chapter 8, discussing the founding of WE LEARN (Women Expanding Literacy Education Action Resource Network), a community that promotes women's literacy as an empowerment tool leading to equity. She asks how this woman-centered group (and other groups subscribing to paradigms that defy those privileged by academia) can remain critical and holistic when ivory tower isolationism contradicts that vision. In Chapter 1, Tannis Atkinson speaks of her journey toward the academy and the ways in which being an adult literacy frontline worker in Canada has been critical in awakening her consciousness as an activist scholar. In Chapter 5, John Garvey, John Gordon, Peter Kleinbard, and Paul Wasserman discuss their journeys into the New York City world of adult literacy as social justice activists. In both chapters, the authors reflect on how policy has contributed to the shrinking spaces in which community struggles continue to remain a site for collective transformation.

As a new academic, I feel that the academy is no longer a home to a polyphony of voices; nor has it especially remained a producer of doubt. Instead, in my experience, academic content and new programs are increasingly driven by neoliberal economic interests (creating degrees based on quick jobs that may or may not exist). An added challenge to the ivory tower is the evermore push to market models for higher education. Academies, in addition to the ivory-tower culture discussed throughout this volume, are being run more and more as corporations (Dei, 2010). With shrinking endowments, panic has set in and the inexorable dance of profit has many swaying to its seductive rhythm. After all, capitalism not only surrounds us but resides within us in terms of what we consider valuable, how we live, and what we believe is possible (Boggs, 2012). In Chapter 7, Sharon Szymanski and Richard Wells describe a labor center situated within the academy along with the rationale for honoring workers' knowledge production. They challenge the vision of education within a neoliberal landscape where higher education has become increasingly instrumentalized and commodified.

So to what extent can we grow and envision a lovelier and more equitable world when we don't have the time and space because we're too busy satisfying the bureaucratic requirements necessary to remain financially competitive with other institutions? Too busy pimping poverty in the creation of new academic programs? Who will tell the emperor he's going to catch cold if he doesn't put on some clothing?

As many of the authors in this volume have pointed out, one contradiction to decentering and nurturing more egalitarian, democratic processes and structures lies in academia's historically deeply entrenched culture that privileges Eurocentric and individualistic interests. This inevitably is at odds with worldviews rooted in collectivity and polyrhythmic ways of thinking and being in the world (Johnson-Bailey, 2001; Johnson-Bailey & Alfred, 2006). Juanita Johnson-Bailey speaks here of the ways in which racism also impacts the narrative of academia. In Chapter 2 she defines what decentering has meant to her as a woman of color within the academy. She also gives examples of how she has worked toward decentering and unpacks what this effort has looked like at different times (based on her positionality). Collective historical memory impacts our constructed realities in ways we may not be conscious of. Historically, what have professors primarily looked like? What are these images based on? Tom Heaney continues to further unpack this thread of the "fluid center" and describes two examples of community academic partnerships from his activist experiences. In Chapter 4, he addresses when it might make sense for the academy and community to work with each other and when hidden agendas might sabotage its success.

As a relative outsider to academic culture, I witness firsthand how power laden, top-down, and opaque many processes are, with landmines and often no room for dissent. Tenure (the true hallmark of one's success in the academy) is an example of a process that has truly been commodified, as well as invariably impacted by issues of power and positionality. In what ways are the least protected/most vulnerable voices (untenured and adjunct faculty) inadvertently silenced because of fear of possible retribution? It becomes irrelevant whether this fear is fulfilled because the result is silencing. How can substantive critique of processes and structures be possible or supported in such a climate? To what extent are there insidious ramifications when vulnerable voices speak up? In Chapter 6, Mechthild Hart describes her identity as a community activist/academic, discussing how she constantly navigates this twin identity, including instances when the two have worked for and against each other. She speaks of our responsibility to collapse binaries and trouble academic scripts that work against democracy, and instead strive to nurture more equitable ebbs and flows of ying/yang.

While actors in this meta-narrative may be more or less well intentioned, the system is one rooted in individualism and competition. Fetishizing and privileging a set of prescriptive guidelines is how one's future/success in the ivory tower is determined. This process is fraught with potential landmines (have I served on the "right" committees? Do the people making decisions about my future know my accomplishments? In Chapter 3, Shivaani A. Selvaraj explores this uneasy navigation between the academy and activism. Selvaraj unpacks her advocacy work with homeless populations and searches for ways that her commitments to social change can reside with and nurture her emerging identity as an academic.

How can we as adult-education activist scholars be part of writing and remaking a new future—one that ensures equitable and democratic access points for multiple voices of different positionalities to access important conversations? What are the ways to most meaningfully speak about how racism impacts scholars of color in academia?

Dissent and a sustained willingness to critique structures and processes are critical to building a truly democratic culture (Heaney, 2010). If this isn't encouraged and supported by those who are most protected in academia, then those who are more vulnerable will be silenced. Whose interests and agendas are protected and ultimately prevail by this dynamic? Those in positions of power within the academy must be especially attentive to subtle ways that voices are being silenced (albeit, inadvertently). Democracy is in the details, in the everyday struggle to foster and sustain a more equitable and inclusive culture where space is made for those whose voices are most marginalized to be heard. However, in a culture that rewards individual accomplishments and where power and positionality are potent, this remains a great challenge. In such a climate, how can we contribute to sustainable conversations aimed at opening up and transforming spaces within the academy—that create more functioning, democratic processes and structures, that fuel political imaginations and remake the world in which we live (Brookfield, 2005; Heaney, 2000)?

The ivory tower is based on (and rooted in) a complex, pervasive, Eurocentric culture. Privileging these linear, hierarchical ways of thinking and functioning can restrict access to democratic openings and efforts. Insular, individualistic cultures that reward competition can stifle and even destroy enthusiasm, morale, and creativity of new scholar practitioners. Bridges to and with communities need to be built and nurtured. Decentering means first of all putting structures in place that support consciousness-raising and honoring different worldviews and perspectives (not only paying these lip service and later exoticizing and othering them). Processes must be transparent and inclusive of all voices, not just the perspectives that reflect dominant points of view. Deeply entrenched individualistic paradigms need to be subverted. Projects that encourage people to work together in groups might be one way to approach this. In addition, finding ways to bridge academic and community knowledge ought to be a priority in subverting individualistic frameworks. This can open up potentially powerful spaces for more collective efforts, rooted in concrete change. Too often, academia is far removed from everyday struggles, which can foster the perception of the academy being elitist, outdated, and irrelevant. Study circles, community activism projects, and participatory action research should be among that which is privileged within this new culture of decentering. Activist scholars, in partnership with experienced faculty, can lead this effort, but they need to be supported in concrete ways. Instead of being neutral or social justice educational sites, higher education culture has mostly become replication of existing dominant power relations in society, complete with privileges conferred along lines of gender, race, class, and other status markers (Johnson-Bailey, 2001). Counter-narratives by activist scholars in the academy have the power to contribute to a larger collective conversation. This dialogue can support a shift in power dynamics and open spaces for more democratic possibilities within academia.

To the extent that the academy should embrace the long view and nurture critical perspectives, to be society's critic and conscience—involved in larger collective conversations rooted in social transformation—then extensive measures must be implemented in order to shift the culture, making it more invitational to different worldviews. Embracing new ways of knowing and being can support academia in becoming bridges to and with other communities, to accessing different, important conversations rooted in change, offering a deep, broad vision of a world that is absent from the myopic present (Faust, 2009).

It is my belief that social justice movements can and should transport us to another space/place, and ultimately enable us to imagine a new world. As adult educators, it is my sense that we have been fortunate to be able to stand on the shoulders of a long line of committed people who have, through their research and practice, made space for us, newer scholar practitioners. It is up to us, working for human and social justice rights (at intersections of adult and community education) to connect with larger movements of our time, and collectively engage in theory building that results in ways we might reframe our practice. I believe current struggles offer us opportunities for resistance, space to grapple with and advance theory and practice. As a former adult literacy education worker, I have been committed to adult education as a potential site for democratic social change. I have continued to grapple with questions like: What would it mean to collectively envision a forward moving, vibrant field that nourishes the collective political imagination of its actors? Who are those actors? How can we live out our commitments rooted in decentering dominant structures in ways that do no harm (even inadvertently)?

I am always in search of inspiration and counter-narratives that can guide me and others in imagining a kind of future we would collectively want to struggle toward. I am reminded that social change is only radical if it promotes struggle and growth at every level—for society, in our intimate and everyday relationships, and internally, within ourselves. Maxine Greene (Personal communication, December 8, 2003) said, "We must learn to labor in the midst of spaces that nurture alternative visions, the possibilities between freedom and imagination—the ability to make present what is absent; to summon up a condition that is not yet." Boggs reminds us that an epistemology of compassion recognizes the ways in which we belong to each other. So, I leave you with her question: What time is it on the clock of the universe? To all of us, who embody the past, present, and future of the field, I ask: How can we begin and sustain the urgent work of radical social transformation . . . decentering, recentering, and reimagining before it's too late?

References

Birkold, M. (2012). Living by the clock of the world: Grace Lee Boggs' call for visionary organizing. *Left Turn.* Retrieved from http://www.leftturn.org/grace-lee-boggs-visionary-organizing

Boggs, G. L. (1998). *Living for change.* Minneapolis: University of Minnesota Press.

Boggs, G. L. (2012). *The next American revolution: Sustainable activism for the 21st century.* Berkeley: University of California Press.

Brookfield, S. (2005). *The power of critical theory.* San Francisco, CA: Jossey-Bass.

Dei, G. (2010). Engaging race, anti-racism, and equity issues in the academy. In J. Newson & C. Polster (Eds.), *Academic callings: The university we have had, now have, and could have* (pp. 170–177). Toronto, Ontario, Canada: Canadian Scholars' Press.

Faust, D. G. (2009, September 6). Crossroads—The university's crisis of purpose. *The New York Times*. Retrieved from http://www.nytimes.com/2009/09/06/books/review/Faust-t .html

Heaney, T. (2000). Adult education and society. In A. Wilson & E. Hayes (Eds.), *Handbook of adult and continuing education* (pp. 559–570). San Francisco, CA: Jossey-Bass.

Heaney, T. (2010). Democracy, shared governance, and the university. In D. Ramdeholl, T. Giordani, T. Heaney, & W. Yanow (Eds.), *New Directions for Adult and Continuing Education: No. 128. The struggle for democracy in adult education* (pp. 69–79). San Francisco, CA: Jossey-Bass.

Johnson-Bailey, J. (2001). *Sistahs in college: Making a way out of no way*. Malabar, FL: Krieger Press.

Johnson-Bailey, J., & Alfred, M. V. (2006). Transformative teaching and the practices of black women adult educators. In E. W. Taylor (Ed.), *New Directions for Adult and Continuing Education: No. 109. Fostering transformative learning in the classroom: Challenges and innovations* (pp. 49–58). San Francisco, CA: Jossey-Bass.

DIANNE RAMDEHOLL *is an assistant professor of adult education and coordinator of the Master of Arts in Adult Learning program (MAAL) in the School for Graduate Studies, Empire State College, New York.*

New Directions for Adult and Continuing Education • DOI: 10.1002/ace

INDEX